T0129138

I Married a

PREACHER

EMMA J. RIGSBY

authorHOUSE®

AuthorHouse™
1663 Liberty Drive
Bloomington, IN 47403
www.authorhouse.com
Phone: 1 (800) 839-8640

Published by AuthorHouse 05/27/2015

ISBN: 978-1-5049-1225-9 (sc)
ISBN: 978-1-5049-1224-2 (e)

Print information available on the last page.

Any people depicted in stock imagery provided by Thinkstock are models, and such images are being used for illustrative purposes only. Certain stock imagery © Thinkstock.

This book is printed on acid-free paper.

Because of the dynamic nature of the Internet, any web addresses or links contained in this book may have changed since publication and may no longer be valid. The views expressed in this work are solely those of the author and do not necessarily reflect the views of the publisher, and the publisher hereby disclaims any responsibility for them.

KJV
Scripture quotations marked KJV are from the Holy Bible, King James Version (Authorized Version). First published in 1611. Quoted from the KJV Classic Reference Bible, Copyright © 1983 by The Zondervan Corporation.

FOREWORD

As you read the following pages, you will get a glimpse of not only the family and life of Jean Rigsby, but you will see that she has also shared her heart. She told me several years ago about the book she was going to write some day, and today I had the privilege of reading the finished product. I intended to read a few chapters per sitting, but once I started I couldn't put it down until the last page!

As you read Jean's story, you will see that she succeeded in honoring the Lord by giving Him the glory for all that He has done in her life. Secondly, she successfully honored her late husband, Brother Billy Rigsby, who was my family's beloved Pastor for many years. Thirdly, her writing will be an encouragement and inspiration to women of all ages who have a desire to serve the Lord, whether as a Pastor's wife, or in any other walk of life.

Jean and I have a unique relationship. She was my Pastor's wife for about 10 years and now I am her Pastor's wife. We have a beautiful friendship and I thank the Lord that He brought the Rigsbys and the Callens together at Eastern Avenue Baptist Church many years ago. My husband and I thank the Lord that "Sister Jean" is still a faithful member of our church and you can be sure that she is loved by all!

My prayer is that God will continue to bless Jean and her family. I love her dearly and I honor her for being such a wonderful example and role model to me.

"...her price is far above rubies."
- Proverbs 31:10b

Mrs. Janet L. Callen
Eastern Avenue Baptist Church
St. Cloud, Florida

DEDICATION

This book is dedicated in loving memory to my beloved husband of 52 years, Billy Ray Rigsby.

We know that all things work together for good to those who love God and are called according to His purpose.

Billy and Emma Jean
Young Love

Billy Ray Rigsby
Age 20

CHAPTER I

I Married a Preacher

Song of Solomon 8:7
Many waters cannot quench love,
neither can the floods drown it:
If a man would give all the substance of his house for love,
It would utterly be contemned.

Emma Jean Woodall (1957)

The words were clear and well-defined, "Young lady, your life will never be the same again." The senior pastor looked down at me over the top of his horn rimmed glasses.

Of course, I was aware that being married to a preacher would not be an easy life. But, I was young, just out of high school and deeply in love. The pastor continued, "Your chosen companion has made a commitment to God. His life is surrendered to ministry wherever God may decide. There will be times when you or your children may become ill. Your husband's calling requires him to minister. You must remember God is number one in his life. "He will not be at your beck and call." Little did I know what that meant! In retrospect, every time the children were ill and I was left alone, the preacher's words came back to remind me.

I listened to the wise words of this dear pastor and nodded my head in affirmation. I did not know what lay ahead. My prince charming had asked me to marry him (rather, told me we were going to get married). The date for our wedding was June 8, 1958, and we were going to live happily ever after.

My "knight in shining armor" arrived at our little country church one Sunday morning. He was dressed in a blue Air Force uniform. His shirt was starched, pants creased and his shoes shining! I later learned that the mirror shined shoes was a Saturday night ritual. They also resulted in an award given him for "Airman of the Year" along with his work ethic. His eyes were black as coal. His hair was as dark as his eyes and not a strand out of place. He had a natural "poof" that would later become a distinction.

The pastor introduced him that morning as a young preacher from North Alabama. I was impressed! He was an Airman 1st Class with the U.S. Air Force, stationed at Pine Castle Air Force base, Orlando, Florida. I came home from church that morning and announced to my mother, "I am going to marry that man one day!" My mother laughed!

(What did she know?) Better yet, he was clueless. He didn't even know I was alive!! (A shy 15 year old in a lavender flowered sundress with two crinolines to help hide her slim figure.) And he certainly did not know that I had a granny who could pray. She knew a God that would move heaven and earth to answer her prayers.

My pastor, Bro. Eli Harris, had known me from a child. I secretly told him I was interested in the young serviceman. Shortly after visiting our church, the military ordered him to change his home base to Homestead in Miami, Florida. Devastated at the news, I told the preacher to ask him if he would write to me. He agreed and our courtship by mail developed. During this time, I learned that he held a position in cryptography. He had a Top Secret clearance and decoded messages for the government. There were times when he would be swept away suddenly to a foreign country. He was not allowed to say when or where he was going. He could not notify family or friends of his whereabouts. Writing to me was of course, off limits. It was stressful for me when I did not hear from him periodically.

I was a junior in high school when our pastor arranged to have a revival meeting. He invited Billy to return from Homestead and conduct the services for us. By this time I felt that I knew him better and was confident that our relationship would grow. My mom and dad had no idea what was going on in my head. On the other hand, I whispered to my grandmother (a wise and godly woman). He's coming to preach our revival.....how can I catch him? I can hear her answer as clearly now as it was then. She quoted Psalms 37:4,5 and said honey, if you will live for the Lord, He will give you the desire of your heart. Later, this verse became a life lesson for me. I claim it as my favorite! I started reading my Bible every night and praying.

During the revival, Billy preached from the heart. He spoke with authority and confidence far beyond his years. His voice rose and swelled in acclamation. He proclaimed his belief in a way that you knew he would never back down. It was his boldness and his stand for Christ that captured my heart. The revival was successful and seven souls were saved. On the final night of the meeting I came forward to rededicate my heart to God. The closing song that evening was "God Be With You Til' We Meet Again." The pastor placed the two of us at the altar while the congregation sang and shook our hands. During this time, God spoke to my heart and said, "One day you will stand at this altar together as husband and wife". Little did I know how quickly that would come to pass.

Billy left that night for the base in Homestead. Later he was sent on a mission to North Africa for six months. We were able to correspond while he was there. I decided to have my picture made at Len's Roben's studio in Orlando, Florida. I explained that it needed to be a "rush order" because my friend was in the military. It was expedited by the photographer and he wrote on the picture, "Priority for Love's Sake". (It is my favorite picture). Billy told me later that after being surrounded by foreign women he loved to come back to his room and actually "fell in love with my picture." I think he was saying, I looked pretty good compared to his surroundings.

He worked in a one room hut located in a desolate tract of the wilderness. It was there he received cryptographic material. It was a lonely time for him. He told of a huge rock in the area where Arabic children came seeking food. They searched for snails in the desert foliage. He would often meet with them and take snacks that he saved from his rations. He called it his prayer rock and would go there to meet with his God.

If you can fall in love with the postal service, I think he did!! Maybe it was his loneliness in a foreign land, but perhaps it was the prayers of a loving grandmother and her 16 year old granddaughter (a petite five foot two, eyes of blue who weighed 98lbs soaking wet). She definitely was NOT a candidate for a locker "pin-up" picture!

In August Billy returned to the states and came to Kissimmee, Florida for a visit. My grandmother who was a pioneer to Florida told me Kissimmee got its name from the Seminole Indians who settled there. An Indian brave quoted to his sweetheart Kiss-A-Me. When Billy arrived this time, he did kiss-a-me. I knew in my heart he was the one.

Later that summer five of my high school classmates asked me to join them on a trip to North Carolina. They were going to a youth retreat, a Southern Baptist encampment called Ridgecrest. We were to travel by train (my first train ride) to meet a youth group from Tampa, Florida. How exciting for a 16 year old teen! The First Baptist Church acquired a bus to transport our group to North Carolina.

Billy agreed to drive me to the train depot. As we sat waiting for the train, he mentioned to me "when we get married?" Not a proposal, just a matter of fact. I was a bit disappointed that he took me for granted. But, why shouldn't he…..after all, I was the one praying to catch him!

The train arrived on time and off we went on an adventure that would result in a life's commitment to the will of God.

My life would never be the same again. I was awed by the beauty of the mountains. The closer we got to Ridgecrest, the higher we climbed, and the closer I felt to God. Majestically, the tall pine trees stretched their branches to the sky. Drifting clouds were low enough to touch yet made you feel your body was on the earth, and your heart was touching heaven. I felt very close to God.

When we arrived at the camp, we were given a cabin and a counselor. We attended classes with workshops in the morning. At noon we ate in the cafeteria. Afternoons were free time, and we rambled around the campus and visited the Book store. The first day of my visit to the store, a book titled "How to be a Preacher's Wife and Like It" caught my eye. I was intrigued and picked it up to read. My mother had given me fifty dollars to last the entire trip. She cautioned me not to over spend because she had only given me enough for food to eat on the way up and back. Every day I went to the book store. Every day I picked up the book and read. Every day I pondered, "Do I have enough money?" Each day I put the book back on the shelf.

At night we had the infamous Dr. R.G. Lee preaching to hundreds of teen agers from across the southeast. He was known for his powerful preaching. "Payday Someday" was one of the greatest sermons ever preached. The last night of our retreat Dr. Lee preached that great sermon. After the sermon an altar call was given for those who felt the calling of God upon their lives. I had accepted Jesus as my Savior as a twelve year old but never committed my life in service to Him. The Holy Spirit tugged at my heart. I eased from my pew down the aisle with a host of other young people. We were handed cards to fill out. One of the questions asked was,

"To what field of service do you think God is leading you"? For me there was no doubt. I felt God was calling me to be a "preacher's wife". What they didn't know was, I already had the preacher picked out! Afterward they took us individually into a counseling session. We made our commitment to God for full time service for life.

Devotion to God for a lifetime! This commitment remains in my heart. Until the day I die, I want to serve Jesus. I want to be His hands, His feet, His voice. The closing service was held around a bon-fire. We sang chorus after chorus, "Where He Leads Me" and "I Have Decided to Follow Jesus". In my heart I knew I was dying to self and committing to God. The future I could not see, but I was allowing God to control me.

I have decided to follow Jesus
I have decided to follow Jesus,
I have decided to follow Jesus,
No turning back no turning back.

Though none go with me, still I will follow,
Though none go with me, still I will follow,
Though none go with me, still I will follow,
No turning back, no turning back.

The girls gathered back in our cabin that night and started singing Happy Birthday to me. My birthday is in December and this was August. Puzzled, I took the gift they handed me. "Happy birthday", my friend said, "we couldn't wait to give you the book you've been wanting in the book store." I cried! This awesome book by Lora Lee Parrott has been invaluable to me in the ministry. It stands in my personal library today.

I returned home from Ridgecrest joyful. My first experience at public speaking came soon afterwards. The pastor, Dr. Amos at First Baptist church in Kissimmee asked our group to speak at the evening service. I volunteered and told of my experience and of my commitment to full time Christian service.

CHAPTER II

Proverbs 18:22
Whoso findeth a wife
Findeth a good thing
And obtaineth favour of the Lord.

In November of 1957 Billy completed his four years in the armed services. He drove immediately to Kissimmee and on the 30th day gave me a diamond purchased at the base commissary.

Several days later he returned to his home in Alabama hoping to find employment. To his dismay everything had changed. He was unable to get a job.

Desiring to complete his education he returned to Florida and with the aid of the G.I. Bill enrolled in college at Florida Baptist Institute and Seminary in Lakeland. My dad, a building contractor, gave him a job in the construction business which would later prove to be monumental in his ministry.

In March of 1958, the Lock Haven Baptist Church where we attended voted to call him as pastor. He was twenty-one years old and on fire for God. He wanted to save the whole world and preached as though it was his last day and yours too. In April he was ordained as a minister of the gospel of the Lord Jesus Christ. Local pastors and ordained brethren laid hands and blessings upon him.

Billy had a vision for the Lock Haven Baptist Church from the day he became pastor. He was like an energizer bunny, working, striving, preaching, praying, visiting, witnessing and reaping, reaping, reaping. The little church with a membership of 22 grew to a membership of over 1,000 in later years.

The Wedding

June 8, 1958, was one of the happiest days of my life! I graduated from high school on June 6th and married two days later. It was a power packed week-end. How my mother survived, I will never know. Our wedding was scheduled for two o'clock Sunday afternoon. Billy, of course, must preach the morning church service and the entire family had to hear him. After the benediction at 12:00 p.m., we hurried home to dress for the wedding. My mother prepared a large lunch and set up tables outside to avoid in- house confusion. It was at least a fifteen to thirty minute drive to the church. Billy's parents, siblings, grandmother and aunt were our guests.

The church we were married in was constructed in 1956 by my dad and his brother in-law. For our wedding my dad made a wooden arch for us to stand under. Mother covered the arch with honeysuckle vine that she gathered from a neighbor's yard. My bouquet was a single orchid with ribbon placed on a white bible. My gown, ballerina length was made of antique lace with an empire waist complimented by velvet ribbon. White satin high heels walked me down the aisle to meet my knight in shining armor.

Friends and relatives witnessed the ceremony of two kids in grown up clothes being brought together as ONE. From that day forward my life would never be the same. The little girl that knew very little about REAL life was on a journey.

The reception was held at our home, a large two story frame house built in 1887 by my great grandfather. My dad inherited the old home place and raised our family where he and his mother were reared. The staircase built by my great grandfather Needham Franklin Bass was decorated with ivy for the tossing of my bouquet. My going away dress (a tailored blue suit) with navy & white polka dotted collar was a size 5. White high heels completed the outfit. I felt like a princess walking down those stairs to join my prince and live happily ever after.

June 8th of 1958 I became the wife of a Baptist Minister. God had it all planned ...but he let me decide when I agreed in 1957 to commit my life to full time Christian service. My dream as a child was to be a nurse, a secretary and a movie star. All of these dreams were fulfilled in my life. I certainly played the role of actress. Every year at Christmas, I performed, sang and directed church programs. I wrote and participated in puppet shows for our Junior Church. For 51 years I played the organ for church services, weddings and funerals. Hollywood was my goal but God made me an actress in a field of His own. The dream of secretary was fulfilled every week and became the most time consuming, (letters, sermons, bulletins, announcements and etc.) As for the nurse, many of my days were spent helping new mothers, comforting older people in nursing homes, visiting hospitals and assuring widows were being cared for at home. God met every dream, maybe not the way I expected but satisfying my every desire.

CHAPTER III

Know therefore that the Lord thy God, he is God the faithful God, which keepeth covenant and mercy with them that love him and keep his commandments to a thousand generations.

Deuteronomy 7:9

Harold and Hazel Woodall with
Emma Jean and Harold Wilson

My childhood was filled with love. Most of my life my two grandmothers lived with us in our two story house. The house was constructed in 1887 by my great grandfather, Needham Franklin Bass. My brother, mother, dad and I were a typical family growing up in the best of times. The mothers were home makers. The dads were the bread winners and the grandmothers were just that, GRAND.

My dad worked with Grandpa Bass and built many of the first railroad depots in central Florida. Later he became a contractor and constructed our local drugstore, library, A & P grocery, physician's offices, and many homes in Osceola County. The original deeds to our home place on Royal Street indicate that it was mortgaged to construct the first "Angebilt" hotel in Orlando, Florida (historic building located on Orange Avenue, contractor Frank Bass).

I was blessed to be born in a prominent family who were among the first settlers in Osceola County. My grandmother, Rosa Myra Monteil Bass was one of the first Librarians at the Hart Memorial Library in Kissimmee. My favorite recollection of "Mama Rose" was sitting at her feet as she read to me. My favorite book was "Uncle Remus". She was proficient in speaking the Negro dialect. My favorite story was "The Tar Baby" and how Brer Rabbit got the last laugh outa Brer Bear.

Mama Rose was petite and precocious. She walked to the library every day (a one mile trek). On Saturdays I walked with her and spent half the day reading books. She always wore a stiffly starched dress, stockings and dress shoes. She taught me to walk with a book on my head for good posture. She stressed the importance of proper stance. Her nick name for me was "sister". She named my brother, "the professor".

Ironically, I became a Sister in the ministry and my brother, a "math professor".

Coming out of the Depression caused most of our community to be in "the same boat" financially. My dresses were made by my mother and grandmother out of cotton feed sacks. We would go to the local feed supply store for corn to feed the chickens. The corn was wrapped in cotton fabrics of many colors and design. I was allowed to pick the sack. My mother always saw that I had the best she could afford. She denied herself of many things. Her desire was to satisfy and make her children joyful.

Mama told me about my first day in school. A September morning in 1946 she braided my hair and dressed me in a feed sack dress. She walked with me to school and instructed me to meet her on Main Street after classes. About 3 p.m. she said she saw me coming hand in hand with the pastor's son from the First Baptist Church. She said I ignored and walked past her as if she were not even there. She wondered later if that little boy influenced my life???

I grew up loving to dance. Mama said it came from daddy. He was known for his skill in "Buck Dancing". She gave me tap dancing lessons. Sometimes we performed on the stage at the local theater. I loved it! Music became my first love. I would listen to records and radio and could sing from memory most of the popular songs of the 50's. My favorite song was from "The Wizard of Oz". Judy Garland sang, "Somewhere Over the Rainbow", a song my heart remembers from youth and treasures through old age.

My grandmother Rosa was chairwoman for the local community house. In the winter when the Northerner's migrated south, she organized and obtained entertainment for them. A program was presented once a week. My first debut was for the winter visitors and of course I sang my favorite song.

In the spring, my girlfriend Judy and I entered a "Hollywood Talent Show". This was a group of talent scouts from California who traveled throughout the United States seeking young artists. They held shows for local talent to perform their skills. Judy and I sang together and won third place. We were given a small gold plated trophy that we passed back and forth for years.

It was the best of times! Some say it was the best of times in American history. Life was simple, an age many call "The Golden Era" when times seemed ideal.

After the Depression and World War II, Americans relished these peaceful years. Our clothes were more gender specific. Girls wore dresses and boys wore jeans. Saddle shoes, bobby socks and rolled up jeans identified teen agers. Poodle skirts were worn to Sock Hops and we danced the Bunny Hop. Life in the fifties was still very strict. The children were seen and not heard. Rock and Roll music was just creeping into the mainstream with radio and television. Elvis Presley, Ricky Nelson, James Dean and Marilyn Monroe were celebrities. You could see them at the Saturday afternoon Matinee for fifteen cents. Blue Waltz and Orange Blossom perfumes caused many allergy attacks in the theater. It was a place for new lovers to meet and hold hands. News reels were boring but had to be seen before the movie. Ushers with flash lights directed us to our favorite seat. The bad kids sat in the balcony and made out.

Sock Hops, Hula Hoops and Cruising were popular. Slang words were chicks, keen cat (cool person) holy cow, squares and back seat bingo (kissing in the back seat). For entertainment on Saturday nights we (a group of boys and girls) would cruise down Broadway. We had one red light in the entire town. When we stopped for the light everyone in the back seat would change seats before the light changed. What fun! However, one night the police decided to curtail our entertainment. They took all of us to the police station for finger printing. We also had to call our parents.

The local cemetery turned into a favorite pastime for the boys. They would hide out with bed sheets and scare the teens that came out to park. Sometimes they posed as good guys who wanted to take girls out for a ride then set up guys in the cemetery to fly across the graves in their sheets.

My Grandmother

Laura Bell Ward with her
5 children and grandchildren.

My mother and grandmother attended the Baptist church in Kissimmee. In the early fifties the pastor was Bro. Eli Harris. My grandmother, Laura Bell Alderman Ward, was a devout Christian and prayer warrior. "Granny" lived in the Boggy Creek Community located in Orange County. She attended church for years at the Mt. Carmel Baptist Church near her home. Strong winds from a hurricane blew the church down. The members were not financially able to rebuild and eventually dispersed to other places. Granny started praying for God to put another church in Boggy Creek. Not only did she pray fervently but she put legs on her prayers. She approached Bro. Harris with a proposal to start holding a prayer meeting in her home once a week. He agreed and from that prayer meeting developed the establishment of the Lock Haven Baptist Church.

My grandmother was known for her powerful praying. Many people would call on her when they were sick. She would drop whatever she was doing and go to their aid. Not only did she pray but she offered her nursing skills as well. Vicks salve, mentholatom, turpentine and a little honey\ whiskey with lemon juice would cure most ailments. My assumption is that her prayers and faith in God were reason for the true healing.

My grandmother greatly influenced my life. She had an aura around her that made you know she "walked with God." Granny's life was not an easy one. Married at age 18 to a man in his 40's, she was widowed for over 30 years. Grandpa died in 1942. He suffered multiple strokes which impaired his memory. He was a prosperous business man but lost everything during the depression era. After grandpa's death Granny was left with little income. She prayed that

God would show her how she could provide for herself. God gave her a dream one night. She saw rows and rows of black eyed peas growing in the back field. She got up the next morning determined to plant black eyed peas in the empty field. From 1942 through 1960 she survived with the income from field peas.

The peas were taken to Orange County's Farmer's Market. People said that granny sold more peas than any other farmer. I'd rather think it was the God who lived within her that drew people to her. When the peas came in everybody went to work. There were hampers of peas all over the porches. A large sheet was placed on the round dining table and the sides were rolled up around the top. All of the shelled peas went into the middle of the table. Later they were sorted and put into sacks for the market.

Grandpa Ward left granny with a big rambling farm house, a few cattle, horses and a yard full of chickens and turkeys. The house was composed of a large living room with a double fireplace between it and the bedroom. Three porches surrounded the house built on brick pillars that sat the house high off the ground. It was an ideal place for the grandchildren to play underneath. The yards did not have grass. The sand was raked with brush brooms. The sugar like sand was white and we spent hours playing. A little water made nice mud balls to throw at each other.

There was no running water in the house. A huge reservoir in the back yard provided rain water for baths and drinking. The bathroom was an "out-house" complete with a Sears and Roebuck catalog used for wishing and wiping.

The grandchildren loved to go to Granny's house in the summer. Cousins spent so many weeks together that we were called kissin' cousins. There would be as many as six to eight children. I will never know how she endured all of us at one time. After we helped Granny in the field, she would reward us by taking us down to the creek. She taught all the grandchildren how to swim though she herself could not swim. A rope was hung from the branch of a tall oak tree. We would grab the rope and swing out over the deepest part of the creek. We did see an alligator occasionally; however, they were as afraid of us as we were of them.

The time we spent on the farm was always fun. There were more critters than people. Snakes were seen often. We left the black snakes alone but if we saw a rattlesnake, Granny would not leave until it was dead. She never seemed to be afraid. One day she stepped into the middle of a five foot rattler coiled. She was working in the pea patch. She screamed for Uncle Orville to come with his hoe. Uncle Orville froze! Granny grabbed the hoe and killed the snake. She always read her Bible when she came home at noon. After lunch on that day she opened her Bible to the scripture below:

Psalms 91:11-14
"For he shall give his angels charge over
thee, to keep thee in all thy ways.
They shall bear thee up in their hands, lest
thou dash thy foot against a stone.
Thou shalt tread upon the lion and adder:
the young lion and the dragon shalt thou trample under feet.
Because he hath set his love upon me,
therefore will I deliver him:
I will set him on high, because he hath known my name.

He shall call upon me and I will answer him:
I will be with him in trouble; I will deliver him, and honour him.
With long life will I satisfy him and shew him my salvation.

I was never afraid when I was with Granny. Her relationship with God was one in a million. I longed to be just like her.

God blessed her with 87 years of fruitful service. When she passed away at home I was with her. As she lay dying, I threw my arms over her and prayed for God to give me her mantel. I wanted the passion she had for God. I wanted to pray and know that my prayers were effective. I wanted to love like she loved.

There were always animals to be cared for on the farm. A milk cow was treasured for the much needed calcium she provided. One night the cow came down sick. She could not move and the veterinarian was called. The cow needed to be turned over every 6 hours. Granny faithfully set her clock and in the cold dark night went out to the edge of the grove to turn over "ole' Betsy." One night she thought she saw Uncle Joe's dog staring at her. The next morning she told him about the incident. He said, "Mama, I don't think that was my dog but we will go look at the tracks." Imagine the surprise when they determined that a panther had tracks all around the cow? The next night guess who turned over old Betsy? Granny, of course!

Granny cooked for all of us. We loved her "fried bread". A mixture of flour, water, and egg fried in an iron skillet. She always had canned vegetables from her garden. There was no refrigerator or freezer. Near the back porch was a guava bush. She loved making guava pie.

At night we all sat on the front porch. There were a few chairs or pea hampers to sit on. We made up ghost stories and told them. One night we had an unexpected visitor. Uncle Orville, granny's brother slipped a sheet over his head and sneaked through the woods. We all saw "it" at the same time and nearly killed each other running into the house. Of course, it was a big surprise when Uncle Orville came back with a sheet in his hand.

The old home place sat on brick pillars. There was ample room to play underneath the house. The boys usually played there, making roads for their wooden trucks and cars. The girls preferred the swing hanging from a camphor tree. It was a huge truck tire tied to a branch with a rope. We also liked climbing the tree. At night the boys would sometimes get under the house. They gathered coarse string and waxed it with bee's wax; then put it through a tin can and wound it tightly, holding the string on each end. It made a weird sound coming from underneath the house. The girls imagined a strange animal after human flesh and it sent us screaming through the house. The boy's loved it and we never caught on to them.

Granny was loved by all the children. She never raised her voice yet spoke with authority. She read her Bible consistently and she lived by what she read. Her eyes were blue; her long hair was faded auburn and came near her shoulders. She brushed it every night. I can vision her now taking down the bun held by a rubber band and hair combs. Her features were plain. She never wore lipstick or make-up. A little face powder when going to church was enough. She made all of her clothes. I never remember her having a "ready made" dress from the store. She was an excellent seamstress. She made clothes for the children and adults. She did not need a pattern. You gave her a picture from a catalog and she would take your measurements and make your dress. She also made quilts, curtains, pillows, etc.

One of my favorite memories was Granny's building fund project. The church was building a new auditorium. Billy gave each person a dollar bill and encouraged them to multiply it for the building fund. Granny decided that she could make and sell aprons. She asked someone to take her "down town" to one of the local restaurants. She talked with the waitresses there and found what type of apron they preferred. They liked the pocket aprons for carrying small articles. Granny started sewing! And sewing and sewing! She made gingham checked aprons in a variety of colors and off to the restaurants she went. It was amazing! Granny was one of the largest contributors to the building fund. After about two months of sewing aprons day and night, Granny said to us, "I think the Lord has overdone this project." She felt like God had given her more than enough aprons!!

Granny was a firm believer in following the rules of God's word. She believed that women should obey their husbands, in the Lord. Soon after Billy and I were married she was visiting with us when he came home from work. I was busy preparing the evening meal. She came and whispered to me, "You need to go and give him some tender, loving care." When I protested, she said to me, "You need to give your undivided attention to your husband. The Bible says that Sarah called Abraham "Lord". Well, I did give him some tender loving care, but I couldn't bring myself to call him Lord, not yet!

One of the greatest lessons I learned from granny was to respect and give honor to your spouse. I have never regretted the fact that HE was the spiritual leader of our household. He made all the final decisions in our home. He was accountable to God. I was allowed to make my thoughts and decisions known, but I gave him the responsibility of making the final judgment. If his call was wrong, I did not say a word. It was between God and him. I reaped the benefits quietly. Honoring your husband is the greatest gift you can give him. I believe before he died, my husband would have given me the moon if it had been possible. He loved me unconditionally because I honored him.

Granny's love for the church was evident. On Saturday she would prepare flowers to sit on the communion table on Sunday. Her home was located less than a mile from the church building. Once a week she walked to the church taking her broom, mop, and pail. She would clean the building and see that the grounds were clean of debris. She was always singing or humming. I do not recall her ever feeling sorry for herself. She spent most of her time helping others. Only eternity will reveal the influence that granny had on the lives of others, especially mine!

CHAPTER IV

My beloved is mine, and I am his:
Song of Solomon 2:16

MY MAN

At the age of fourteen I joined a local youth group (comprised of young people in churches of surrounding counties). We met on Friday nights once a month at local churches. It was then that I found myself attracted to preachers. They fascinated me and perhaps it was God's way of leading me in that direction.

Billy was different from all the rest. When he got up to speak, it was with authority. He did not waste time with introductions. He got right to the point. He later told me his motto: Stand up-Speak up-and Shut up! And that he did. He never preached long but what he said counted. Many people said that he could say more in fifteen minutes than most preachers could say in an hour.

Before we were married Billy came up from Homestead for a visit. Mother made a bedroom for him on the second floor of our home. She later named it "Elijah's" room. It was a Saturday afternoon that I will never forget. He was upstairs and I was downstairs watching the "American Bandstand". A group of the kids from our high school were appearing on the show. I was so involved in watching the dance routines that I did not see him start down the stairs. He pointed his right arm forward with the index finger at me quoting scripture,

"Love not the world, neither the things that are in the world. If you love the world, the love of the Father is not in you." He did not approve of my dancing or my friends behavior. I got the message! I stopped dancing but I never got over my love for it.

I loved his straight forwardness. He never left you any doubt on what he believed. You were not wondering "Now what did he think on that subject?" Over the 52 years we were married there was only one time that he was mistaken for anyone other than a preacher. It was the pleasant way he greeted you. He always made people at ease, comfortable. His personality was often filled with wit. His memory was sharp. He told the same stories over and over never forgetting ALL the details. In the fifty two years of marriage, I never tired of hearing him preach or tell his stories. He was a master story teller. He would have you laughing one minute and crying the next.

My favorite sermon was on the parable of the lost sheep:

Luke 15
What man of you, having an hundred sheep, if he lose
one of them, doth not leave the ninety and nine in the
wilderness, and go after that which is lost, until he find it?
And when he hath found it, he layeth it
on his shoulders, rejoicing.

He described the shepherd returning home with the lost lamb on his shoulders, depicting the love of the shepherd. He wrapped the sheep around his neck on both shoulders.

Billy's compassion for people came from his childhood experiences. He was raised on a farm in the hills of North

Alabama. Sand Mountain was his boyhood home. His mother, Johnnie was given a boy's name at birth. She could do just about anything a man could do and sometimes better. She once told me that Billy was almost born in the "cotton field". They were "share croppers" and the farm had to be maintained. She carried a pick sack on her back and she would pick more cotton than the laborers. Her back in later years was bent over due to the years laboring in the cotton fields. Johnnie was a woman of strong faith and had a great influence on Billy. She taught her boys to work hard. All three of them were great to help in the kitchen and with other house hold chores.

I always loved Saturdays when Billy would be home. He pitched in and helped with the house cleaning. However, he did the "white glove" test. It had to be perfect and you can be sure he would inspect our jobs. He also loved cleaning the car. My dad would say, "Billy will let the grass get knee high, but that car will be clean." I do not think he ever let the grass get knee high but he did love his car clean! He was meticulous, perhaps a perfectionist. But, when he had a job to do, you knew it would be done right.

His clothes also were meticulous (stiffly starched white shirts with NO wrinkles). A pressed suit from the dry cleaners, creases in the pant legs, bright necktie usually red and pocket hankie to match; he stood out in a crowd. Not to forget his shoes shined with a cotton ball and shoe wax. I loved my man! He made me so proud! I did not have to worry about how he would look even when he was not in a suit and tie. He managed to look picture perfect in a pair of denim jeans.

When our church had picnics in the woods, he always wore jeans, a western shirt and his "Seminole" hat (rep. Florida State Seminoles). Someone asked him one day how much his hat cost. He replied, "Just over 20,000.00 dollars!" (Tuition for his baby girl's entrance to Florida State). He was proud of that hat and of her.

OUR THREE DAUGHTERS

His daughters were the joy of his life. Lisa the eldest and most like him {perfectionist} completed college after the births of her two boys. She worked a full time job in the county school system and took night classes in Lakeland, Florida. She graduated Suma Cum Laude from Florida Southern college. Several years later she received a Master's degree, also Suma Cum Laude from St. Leo University. She taught school several years before moving to the County Office where she now holds the position of Director of Personnel.

Lisa Lynn Rigsby
9-13-60

Lisa was born in September of 1960. She was three weeks premature due to hurricane "Donna" that hit our town on Saturday before her birth on Tuesday night. The local hospitals sent out warnings for women in their ninth month to be on guard as the low pressure would sometimes bring on contractions.

Billy was preaching a revival at the now "Landmark Baptist Church" in Haines City, Florida. It was approximately a 60 mile drive. The hurricane had caused severe damage. There were so many trees and limbs across the roads that we were not able to get to church on Sunday. Billy helped the city workers clear the roads on Monday and Tuesday. There were pot holes in the roads from all the rain. Driving was difficult and riding was rough. He preached that night by kerosene lanterns. The electricity was off for three days in our town and longer in Haines City. On the way home on Tuesday evening we collided with several pot holes which shook me out of my seat. I told him to take it easy or we might just have a baby. Sure enough, that night about 2:00a.m., labor began. We rushed to Orange Memorial Hospital in Orlando. September 13, 1960 our beautiful baby girl was born. Lisa Lynn Rigsby was the prettiest baby in the nursery. Black hair, brown eyes, 6 pounds and 6 ounces, an adorable child. We thanked God for His loving kindness and we dedicated her life to the One who gave her to us.

Billy kept preaching the revival that week and the next. The meeting was so successful they continued for two weeks. Souls were saved, hearts revived and on the last night we took our baby girl to her first church service. The members showered us with gifts but our greatest was the child in my arms. She was our gift from God. Only a mother who has experienced the loss of a child can enjoy the love of her replacement. I sometimes wonder why God took our first child only to be reminded that the baby I long for is waiting for me in heaven. What joy it will be to hold the child I never touched.

When Lisa was a year and three months old we had a local photographer make her picture. She posed with a stuffed Coca Cola Santa Clause. The photographer thought she was cute enough to place in the local paper. She made the front page just before Christmas in a red jumper, white blouse and pointed fur hat.

I had always loved dolls as a little girl. Lisa was my little doll. I loved her! I sang to her! I rocked her! And I bathed her. One day the doctor said to me at her three month check up, "Mrs. Rigsby, her skin is too dry. How often do you bathe her?" I had to admit to him that she was not allowed to get dirty.

Lisa was very independent. She wanted to do things herself. She did not want anyone to sleep with her. She learned quickly and was walking by nine months. She was the most obedient child. Billy was harder on her because she was the oldest. My mom always took up for her and favored her because she felt she was punished too much. She took the blame many times for other children and her siblings. Lisa was always at the top of her class scholastically. She was consistent and diligent in completing assignments. She loved music and learned to play the piano.

Kathy Ann Rigsby
September 12, 1962

On the eve of Lisa's second birthday her baby sister, Kathy was born. Lisa was excited more over her sister than her first tricycle. Kathy's birth was two weeks earlier than expected. I awakened Billy that my labor had started. To add to my anxiety, he took the time to shave, bathe and look his very best. By the time we arrived at Orange Memorial they did not have time to prep me. She was born one hour later. All seven pounds nine ounces were precisely made to order. Black hair, green eyes and beautiful, her pictures are very similar to Lisa. Mother helped name her as we had chosen a boy's name. Kathy Ann seemed to fit. Mama chose Kathy and I added Ann for my best friend in high school.

Kathy was blessed with nine months of colic. She cried and cried and cried. At three months I stopped breast feeding thinking the milk did not agree with her. We tried paregoric, asitifidity and even a rabbit's foot around her neck. Nothing worked! She would only let me or my grandmother hold her. I did most of the house work with her on my hip. She was definitely a mama's girl. Kathy was shy but after she overcame the colic was a very happy baby. She smiled so much people at church nicknamed her "smiley". When I tied her wisp of hair up with a bow, they called her "Bam, Bam".

When Kathy was nine months old we moved into our new house on Royal Street. My uncle Addison Bodiford constructed the three bedroom, two bath home for us. We had a large living room, Florida room, kitchen and dining room. A brick front with a garage, this house was a dream come true.

At two years of age Kathy and Lisa became inseparable. They loved playing together. Dolls, doll houses, miniature stove and matching refrigerator were housed in a large back yard play house that my dad built for them. He constructed it in his barn and when it was finished realized it was too big to move. After a considerable time and wanting to get it in place for Christmas, he made ski's to fit behind his truck and skied it over to our house across the street. The same year Billy's parents came down and brought the girls matching doll buggies. They loved to stroll their dolls over to Grandmother's house. Then they would take a break on the porch swing. Of course, mama always had cookies and treats for them.

Lisa was always the leader and she directed all the games. One day she decided to play barber shop. She trimmed Kathy's bangs right up to the scalp. Kathy never complained. She was too small to realize how pitiful she looked. She always did what Lisa wanted her to do, even if it was wrong.

When they were older in middle school they became bored one Halloween night. I suggested to them they could "roll" my friend Barbara's house. How could I possibly know the Chief of Police would drive down Oak Street on October 31st? Kathy escaped; however Lisa was detained by the Chief of Police (a friend of ours). Chief Watford caught her by the arm and said, "Young lady, what is your name? "When she told him, he said, "Please tell me you are not Billy Rigby's daughter! Her reply, "My mom said it would be fun!"

When Kathy entered school, Lisa helped her with home work. I often told her not to call Kathy stupid because she was going to give her a complex. Lisa was smart and expected her younger sibling to be at her level. In high school the roles reversed. Lisa was known as Kathy's sister because of her popularity as a cheer leader. Lisa said she ended up with the complex not Kathy. My favorite memory of Kathy's humility came in her Junior year. She had a friend who wanted to be on the cheer leading team. Kathy spent hours working with her. She told me one day that she had prayed for her friend to be chosen even if it meant that she did not make it. Kathy did not make the team that year but her friend was chosen. She was disappointed but her popularity excelled because of her humility. The next year she was chosen as a candidate for home coming queen. We could not afford to buy her a gown. She found a pattern, and I made her evening dress. A strapless formal made of white organza (a delicate fabric). The skirt had fourteen gores that were ankle length. Fully lined, it was two dresses in one and I was never so happy to finish a garment. She was beautiful that night and though she came in second place, we were very proud of her.

Kathy, the middle child, attended Lake Sumter Community college and later became the Assistant Vice President of Loans for Bank of America. Later, after moving out west she worked for Barrick Gold Mines in Elko, Nevada

as Administrative Secretary to the President. Her position of ten years was interrupted by the birth of her first child. Having been barren for over 10 years, she promised God if He would give her a child she would quit work and devote her time to raising him in the admonition of the Lord. God honored her prayer and gave them a son. She has been true to her promise.

AnaRae, the baby girl was named by her father. After her birth, I related to Billy that it was only fair that he name the last and final daughter. He chose the name AnaRae. I did not like the name and cried over it, so did Lisa and Kathy. Later we learned that he named her for a girl that he had known from high school. He did tell us that she was a beauty queen. We felt a little better...... Later, she became "our AnaRae".

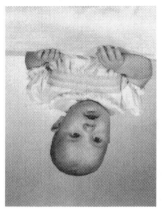

Anna Rae Rigsby
January 23, 1969

AnaRae was a "surprise baby" and she didn't come cheap. Billy had been working with the City of Kissimmee

as Purchasing Agent. Because the church was experiencing phenomenal growth he had decided to step out in faith and quit his job of ten years with the city. It was a major leap of faith. He called our family together for a conference. He explained to the girls that daddy's salary was going to be reduced. Financially, he could not continue to give them what they had become accustomed. But, he assured them God would supply our needs and they must learn to be content with what God provided for us. The most important thing was; daddy was going to be able to spend more time doing the work God called him to do.

Billy decided to take college classes in Lakeland and since Lisa and Kathy were both in school, I opted to go with him. We enjoyed the time together and increased our knowledge of the word. He was also very busy with revivals that year.

AnaRae's conception was truly a God timed one. Our faith was both tested and proved during my pregnancy and her birth. I will never forget Billy's response to my positive pregnancy test. "Are you sure? How could this happen? Well......he knew it wasn't the postman (he was ancient)! We received the news on a Wednesday and Wednesday night was business meeting at the church. We were blessed with a dear old deacon who was always negative. The church had purchased an old school bus to restore and put on the road. The junior church was growing and a bus was needed to provide transportation for children. Billy believed that anything the church put on the road should be in excellent condition (inside and out). He always said God deserved the best we had. Obviously, the old deacon felt we could get by cheaper. Well.......that night was not a good business

meeting. Billy lost his cool with the deacon and said, "this church will not put any junk on the road for Jesus." Always trying to make peace, I sought him out afterward, to tell him that the preacher was distressed over another baby on the way.

We finally decided, "WE are going to have a baby, we have "NO" insurance but God owns the cattle of a thousand hills and He will provide!" And He did. When I went for my visit to the obstetrician he waived my monthly visits because Billy was a pastor. The hospital bill was the only charge we would need to pay.

Lisa and Kathy were precious little girls. They were obedient, played well together and never gave me a minutes' trouble. They were bashful and hid behind my skirt when introduced to people. There was a little boy in our church that was so.....cute. He was friendly and outspoken. I admired this child and was so sure that my baby was going to be the boy we had always wanted that I prayed for a child like Dewayne. Little did I know what I was asking for......

On January 23, 1969 one month before her due date, our AnaRae struggled to be set free. Lisa and Kathy both were sick with the mumps. Their little jaws were puffed up like chipmunks. When I woke up to care for them in the night suddenly my water broke. Totally unprepared for the event and worried about the premature birth, we raced again to the Orange Memorial Hospital in Orlando. The labor was long and lasted until the evening of the next day. Her breathing was shallow due to her prematurity. The physician told me later that he had been in twice to administer CPR. After we brought her home she continued with choking spells. When she was six weeks old special x-rays were given because of breathing difficulties. A tiny six pounds, she was handled with the greatest care. She was adored by her older sisters. Billy's mother came and helped care for her. It was a blessing to have her in our home. She enjoyed Lisa and Kathy so much. Billy loved having her visit as she was the world's best cook. Her biscuits were made with lard and buttermilk and so tasty.

With all the tender loving care AnaRae soon began to overcome her difficulties. She flourished on breast milk and by six months weighed 25 pounds. Billy nicknamed her "thunder thighs". A happy baby, she was never still. She would keep up with the entire household. She stayed up as long as there was a light on anywhere in the house.

By the time she was two years old, she was talking our ears off. There were never any secrets in our house after AnaRae was born. She told them all: to neighbors, friends and relatives, anyone who would listen. By this time, Lisa and Kathy considered her more of a nuisance than a pleasure. She required far too much attention. I remember one incident when I asked them to take her for a ride in the stroller. They were quick to obey. I watched from the window as they started taking turns pushing the stroller however when they tired of pushing, they would both give a great big shove and AnaRae and the stroller went sailing down the street.

However, they defended her when they thought it was necessary. I hired a baby sitter to stay with the three of them one evening. When I arrived home they were very upset and told me," Mom, you should never have that baby sitter again. She made AnaRae stay in her bed and let her cry for hours." Later I learned that the baby sitter thought AnaRae was spoiled. Needless to say, I am sure that was the case but the girls had never seen her so heartbroken. They couldn't stand the crying.

AnaRae's talkative behavior was many times embarrassing. When she was about four years old she answered the door bell to a man I did not know. She said to him, "Oh no, you are wearing that same old yucky shirt again." The man was a friend of Billy. I had not met him. AnaRae often went with her daddy to places around town. Billy loved cars and often visited used car lots. By the time she was six years old she could tell you the make and model of most automobiles on the highway. Of course, her daddy loved that. Once at a Cadillac dealership the salesman was trying to tell Billy how to differentiate between a 1982 and 1983 car. AnaRae spoke up and told them it's the grill on the front.

AnaRae's desire to be the next "Barbara Walters" was not fulfilled. Despite our forecast of her becoming a Used Car Saleswoman, she chose teaching. After completing her education at Florida State University in Tallahassee, Florida she began her first job of teaching at the Gateway High School, Kissimmee, Florida. In 2009, she received a Master's degree from the University of South Florida. She has taught high school English in central Florida for twenty-four years.

CHAPTER V

A Heavenly Gift

And we know that all things work together for
good to them that love God, to them who are the called
according to his purpose.
Romans 8:28

We had been married just three months when a morning
sickness came over me. The illness continued despite my
treatment for nausea. When my mother suggested I might
be pregnant, I was elated. Starting a family was "a dream
come true." My first visit to the doctor confirmed our
suspicions; however, he noted that I had a cervical infection.
He cauterized the area and warned me that I might miscarry.
The pregnancy was difficult. I was sick from morning till
night and gained only a few pounds. My physician told me
that if I carried the child it would be doubtful that it would
be full term.

March 9, 1959 was a beautiful spring day. The birds
were chirping in the trees. Pink azaleas' were blooming
around the old oak tree that was planted in the late 1800's.
My mother had offered to help me with the laundry. I was
hanging clothes in her back yard when I felt a pain in my
lower back and later realized that early labor was beginning.
Doctor's made house calls in those days. My mother put me
into bed and then called our family physician. He came and
administered a shot to stop the labor and ordered complete

bed rest. The next person to be notified was Granny. She was the next best thing to a doctor.

The following week was one of the worst of my life. The medication the doctor prescribed only dulled the continuous pain in my lower back. When labor would start, I tried to hold back to prevent the baby from coming. When I did, the pain only increased. On Monday March 16th the pain was unbearable. Billy called the ambulance service and they raced me to the Orlando General Hospital. The facility was small, and I remember them taking me on the stretcher up a narrow stairway to the second floor. They admitted me into a ward with several older ladies. The nurse came in to take my vitals, and I kept telling her that my baby was coming. Finally, she pulled back the cover and saw a tiny head popping out. Immediately, they rushed me to delivery. There was no prep time, our tiny little girl was born. "One pound and thirteen ounces," I heard the doctor say. The nurse asked if she should hook up the incubator. I saw the doctor shake his head, no. As loud as I could, I asked them to please go and ask my husband to pray. The next thing I remember was waking up to a tiny cry in the nursery next to my room. She was alive! God had answered prayer. The next two days will forever be like yesterday in my heart. I was filled with an overwhelming love. What an amazing feeling to be a mother! A part of me and a part of Billy, our child, together made by and through the hand of Almighty God.

On the morning of the second day I was allowed to see her. Placed in the nursery window in a small incubator was a baby. She would have fit in a shoebox. Her tiny head covered in black hair that curled around her ears. She was beautiful, fragile, like an angel. We will call her Angela Jean, I determined. I stayed with my nose pressed against the window until the nurse ordered me back to my room. My room that afternoon had rays of sunshine that shined from wall to wall; beams of sunlight suddenly taking over the room. It was a moment of serenity that encompassed me totally.

Afterward, I wrote a letter to my mother-in-law trying to describe to her my incomprehensible happiness. I wanted to name her Angela because she looked like an angel to me. I dreamed during the days of her labor of seeing a baby with wings floating above me.

Later that afternoon I learned that my moment of serenity had been the coming of angels. Through my room and into the nursery they came, leaving their aura of sunlight streaming. The doctor came in with his white starched coat gleaming. "Your baby just died, I'm sorry." There was no one with me, and I was left with the news until I could get to a telephone. A thousand questions went through my head that afternoon. Why was God punishing me? What have I done to deserve this? Women are aborting babies every day but I wanted mine, why? This is not fair! God why?

I went home that day to an empty nursery. A little cedar chest filled with baby clothes made by my mother. I cried until I could cry no more. Billy went to the funeral home to select a casket. A tiny white one with gold trim, it was perfect. We had to borrow money, three hundred and fifty dollars, from my parents to bury her. I did not go to the funeral. It was a grave side service held by our friend Rev. Hickey. Mother told me that Billy took it hard. It was hard for mama too. She experienced the loss of her first child who was stillborn. There were only a few family members and friends who attended.

I blamed God for a long time. I could not understand why He would take my child while there were other people who had children and then abused them. I remember going over to my neighbors one day. She was ironing her little girls ruffled dress and complaining about the inconvenience. I went home thinking, "How I wish I had a little girl. I would enjoy ironing her clothes."

Perhaps we'll never know why our baby was chosen to die so soon. I can see now that God used our sorrow to enable us to comfort others. God does not make mistakes! Every sorrow is for a purpose and can be used to glorify God. I do know, God used our very sad event to draw us closer together as husband and wife. I will never forget the first Mother's Day after our Angela died. Billy went to town and bought me a dress. He said I was still a mother even though our baby was not with us. I will never forget that thoughtful act that endeared me to him.

My nightmare did not end that spring. Because of the premature birth and the doctor's concern for keeping the baby alive, my physician failed to properly care for me. For several months after her birth I suffered with profuse bleeding. I was referred to a Dr. Courtland Berry in Orlando. He was a surgeon who had been studying cancer research. This kind, compassionate doctor took me aside after examination and testing. He indicated to me that the test results showed the beginning of cervical and perhaps uterine cancer. He would operate immediately and would try to save my uterus if possible. Not only was I devastated over losing my child, but now I was faced with the possibility of never having another.

The night before my surgery, I signed papers giving Dr. Berry the authority to do a complete hysterectomy if necessary. Billy and my parents went home and prayed. He told me later that he spent the entire night on his knees. To God be the glory, the next day Dr. Berry was able to save my uterus and eradicate the infection around it. Never underestimate the power of prayer. My hearts' desire was to bear children and bring them up in the admonition of the Lord. As Hannah prayed, I prayed:

> *I Samuel 1:10, 11,*
> *And she was in bitterness of soul,*
> *And prayed unto the Lord,*
> *And wept sore.*
> *And she vowed a vow,*
> *And said, O Lord of hosts,*
> *If thou wilt indeed look on the affliction*
> *Of thine handmaid and remember me and*
> *Give unto me a child,*
> *Then I will give him unto the Lord*
> *All the days of his life.*

May I tell you that God honored Hannah's prayer and He honored our prayer. The following year on September 13, 1960 I gave birth to another beautiful baby girl. She was given to God before she was born. She was taken to church before she was two weeks old. She was taught to obey God is better than to sacrifice. She was taught that obedience to God is the key to blessing. This precious child accepted Jesus as her Savior at the age of seven. A tiny little toddler at age three, she opened her purse and took change out. She then walked up to the communion table in the middle of her daddy's sermon and placed her money in the offering plate. To this day, she is known for her heart of giving.

CHAPTER VI

The First Year

The first year of our marriage was filled with ups and downs. I had a small savings account that mom and dad had put back for my education. Billy had numerous jobs but nothing permanent. Our best man Julius talked him into buying a big truck with my savings. The plan was to go into the produce business. They would take water melons from Florida and haul them to Georgia to sell. When they got to Georgia the Florida water melons looked liked cantaloupe compared to Georgia's rattlesnake melons. They practically gave away the melons or traded them for peaches. They brought home a truck load of peaches. Most of them went bad before they could be delivered. And so...........that one trip ended the produce business. God sometimes lets us learn lessons the hard way. We were able to sell the truck and take back the savings.

Our first home was an apartment on Royal Street just five blocks from my parents. Billy got a night job with Martin Marietta. We lived behind a convenience store and the noise from the traffic was unbearable. Trying to sleep in the day was difficult especially with no air conditioning. His nerves were on edge and mine too. We had a major disagreement, and I went home for three days. I don't think he would have made up if my dad had not gone and talked to him. He always had trouble accepting advice because he was never at fault??? At least, I thought so...

Money was a big problem…there was never enough. Our rent was $60.00 a month; groceries were $20.00 dollars a week. We always had a car payment. We had one vehicle, and he used it for transportation to work. I learned early on that his favorite past time was trading cars. When we married he had a 1952 Chevrolet (hard top). It gave the appearance of a convertible. I loved that car and cried when he sold it. I soon learned that crying was useless. If I had cried every time he traded cars it would have made a river of tears.

The church was not financially able to have a full time pastor. He was always able to find secular work. He was not afraid to dig ditches, pour concrete or drive a U-haul. He finally landed a good job with the city of Kissimmee. He went to work for Mr. H. Jones, director of Public Works. Later that job resulted in a position in the city hall as purchasing agent for the City of Kissimmee. He held this position for ten years.

Little is Much When God is in It

In 1969 we began construction of a 450 seat auditorium for the Lock Haven Baptist Church. The original auditorium where we were married would seat 150 and our congregation was growing rapidly. Billy's vision for the church was big. I will never forget the long "dinner shed" that was built for our "All day Sunday meetings and Dinner on the grounds". The church originally had "out houses" for bathrooms. Billy's first building project was to tear these down. He would tease me every Sunday morning, driving up close to them and revving the motor. "One of these days they are coming down", he'd say. I was always afraid he might do it and they would be occupied. After the new bathrooms Sunday School class rooms were erected. Now, it was time for a new auditorium.

The obstacles that followed were yet unseen. God had blessed Billy with many jobs. This was the greatest. Never underestimate the power of Satan when there is a place of worship being constructed. We had one acre of land. We had it surveyed and the adjacent property owners objected. God resolved that issue. The next problem was a permit to build the building. Orange County building codes required a certain amount of land for adequate parking. We did not have enough land! Billy asked the church to have an all night prayer meeting before he went to the board of commissioners. On the day of the meeting, a man who owned the adjacent property spoke on our behalf. Unknown to us, he offered to give us enough land to provide adequate parking. You see, God wanted a house of worship. God put it on the heart of Dr. Crews to give us the land. God will make a way when there is no way! Prayer changes things!

In June of 1969 a new auditorium was completed. The best was yet to come. We started broadcasting our Sunday morning services on a local radio station. The program brought people, the church experienced phenomenal growth in the next five years. We bought a school bus to transport children to Sunday school and church. This led to a children's church service which led to a fleet of ten busses. A minister of music was obtained, and a Junior Church director was put on staff. There was an excitement that was contagious. Sinners were being converted and back-sliders revived.

In 1972 our music minister resigned. The church prayed and God sent a young man full of energy and love for God. Bro. Tommy Morris was a dynamic singer who became a lifelong friend. He and his wife Jacque had their first child, Bryan, during their ministry with us. A house for them became the next project for the church. A new house was constructed on Royal Street. Billy and Tommy were inseparable. They both had a love for God, passion for lost souls and a lust for automobiles.

Tommy organized a group of singers and formed a church quartet. (David Mutter, bass guitar, Jerry Pugh, lead guitar, Frances Mutter, alto, Tommy Morris, lead, Jimmy Fisher, tenor, James Sawrey, bass). The quartet and church choir were invited to perform for churches around the state of Florida and in Georgia. This led to prayer for a Greyhound bus. The preacher and I had gone to a conference in Lynchburg, Virginia. The Liberty Baptist church had several of these and we decided if God would provide for Liberty then He would provide for Lock Haven. We started praying and then shared our prayer with the church. Billy started looking for a bus and found one in Mississippi. A wealthy man in our church offered to purchase the bus and give it for a tax write off. He and Billy went to Mississippi and drove a Continental Trailway bus home. It was large enough to transport the quartet, choir, instruments, and it was air-conditioned. The bus provided transportation for many years thereafter. The laughter and music that filled that bus will forever be ingrained in my mind. God heard our prayers.

While in Lynchburg, Virginia we met the famous Dr. B.R. Lakin. He was preaching for Dr. Fallwell and staying at our motel. He and Billy would chat during breakfast. Billy asked him if he had any openings for revivals. At that time he was booked in advance for three years. When we returned home we learned that Dr. Lakin's nephew had been coming to our church and lived in our area. The next year we were able to get Dr. Lakin for a meeting due to a cancellation of one of his meetings and the influence of his nephew Jim.

What a revival we had that week. Dr. Lakin was one of the first "Circuit riding preachers in West Virginia." The stories he told kept us spell bound. A master orator, he had you laughing one minute and crying the next. Our choir had a black board and one night we found his signature under this phrase: "Stand on the word of God and the God of the word will stand by you"! I memorized this and have never forgotten it.

Our middle daughter, Kathy, was converted during this meeting. Kathy had a tender heart, but she also had a stubborn streak. Lisa had tried witnessing to her but she was angry because she had heard her daddy say that God did not hear the prayer of an unbeliever. She decided there was no need for her to pray if God wasn't going to listen. Thank God, the Holy Spirit and the words of B.R. Lakin touched her and she gave her heart to Jesus.

Billy loved Dr. Lakin. During that week they shared and Dr. B. R. gave Billy some valuable advice. Billy felt impressed to take him to the local department store, and buy him a new suit. He felt honored that he had been able to spend time with this powerful man of God.

In 1972 the church honored us with a trip to Israel. We flew from Orlando to Kennedy Airport in New York. From New York it was an eight hour flight to Germany then a shorter flight to Haifa. An unbelievable ten days followed. In Jerusalem we visited one of our missionaries on Sunday morning. Awakened early to sounds outside our hotel, we viewed a camel covered with new fallen snow. What a surprise for me (a native Floridian who had never seen snow). On our way to church that morning I was so excited about the snow that my feet kept going out from under me. After picking me up several times, I got a lesson on how to walk on icy ground. We were transported to the mission church in a local bus that had been used Saturday to transport chickens to the market place. The smell caused us to put down the bus windows which blew ice and snow in our faces. I had never been that cold in my life. The church had marble floors and one wood burning heater. The cold was uncomfortable but the excitement in my heart far outweighed the discomfort. That afternoon we visited Bethlehem. The next few days brought a boat ride on the Sea of Galilee. Surrounded by mountains, this was the most beautiful place I had ever seen. We visited the garden tomb and walked the Via del a Rosa where Jesus carried the cross to his Crucifixion. By far the most spiritual place was the tomb where He was laid. We sang there and the glory of the Lord could be felt in our midst.

The Bible came alive to me during our visit to Israel. When I read the word I can envision the place. God has blessed me many times; this trip was one of the best. Arriving back in New York and viewing the Statue of Liberty made us grateful. Our trip was ended with a group from the church who met us at the Orlando International airport. A reporter from the local news media interviewed Billy. We felt like celebrities' when the paper came out that week.

CHAPTER VII

A Saint Goes Home

2 Peter 1:13-15

*Yea, I think it meet, as long as I am in this tabernacle,
to stir you up by putting you in remembrance; knowing
that shortly I must put off this my tabernacle, even as
our Lord Jesus Christ has shewed me. Moreover I will
endeavor that ye may be able after my decease to have
these things always in remembrance.*

In 1974 my beloved Grandmother became ill with leukemia. She had never been in a hospital. Her children were all born at home. God blessed her with 87 years of good health. She had a couple of episodes of pneumonia. At that time the doctor came to the residence and prescribed medication. That is my only recollection of any illness. She often would have a cold and cough in the winter but she doctored herself with home remedies. One was something called "Hadacol". It apparently had some alcohol in it and she would get a bit tipsy.

In March she became bedridden and the doctors said to keep her comfortable. She was hospitalized twice and given blood. On the night that she died my mother called us about 2:00 a.m. We gathered around her bed and offered prayers. She left this world as peacefully as you could imagine. As I stood there my thoughts were: Who is going to pray for us now? Granny was our intercessor. She connected with God.

She had a little song that God gave to her whenever her prayers were affirmatively answered. She could not sing it any other time. It was a God given song for her alone.

Shortly after her death, I heard a song called, "I've Got More to go to Heaven For". It was my comfort song for many years afterwards.

> I've been on my way to heaven,
> For a long, long time
> And many things have happened
> That's clouded up my mind.

God used this song to help me through my grief. The days were long and lonely, but her legacy lives on. What a powerful influence she had on so many people. There were over four hundred people who attended her service. Her funeral was uplifting. A celebration of her home going better describes the service. Tommy and Jacque Morris returned for the funeral from Arkansas. We all met that night at our home on Royal Street. We sang hymns and gave testimony to her.

I will never forget one of Granny's statements regarding funerals. She was always one to put church above anything else. If she had company; she told them they could go to church with her or they could stay at home and wait for her return. The worship hour was more important!

Whenever Billy was in revival she was the first to hop in the car. She loved him and she also loved the gospel that he preached. She would take his side in any argument. There was a member of her family that died. The funeral was going to be held on a Sunday. When asked if she was going to attend, she responded with the scripture: "Let the dead bury the dead, I am going to serve the Lord."

Granny was buried in the Lock Cemetery with her departed family. Laura Bell Alderman Ward was the "most influential person in my life".

The legacy of Laura Ward causes me to be cognizant that:

There is only one life -It soon shall pass,

Only what is done for Christ

Will last.

CHAPTER VIII

Church Trouble

Ephesians 4:31, 32
Let all bitterness, and wrath, and anger, and clamour and
evil speaking, be put away from you, with all malice:
And be ye kind one to another, tenderhearted,
forgiving one another, even as God for Christ's sake hath
forgiven you.

We learned early on in our marriage that problems exist
in churches. There were problems over petty circumstances,
personal differences and doctrinal principles. Our first
difficulty came over church doctrine. There were members
of the church who believed that "Foot Washing" should be
a church ordinance. This was derived from the scripture
where Jesus washed the disciple's feet. The church doctrine
holds "The Lord's Supper" and "Baptism" as the only two
ordinances. We addressed the issue with several of our
church Elders from Lakeland present at the meeting. Our
efforts failed at convincing these disgruntled members. They
left the church and started a Free Will Baptist Church.

Problematic persons usually gather a crowd. Then the
problem spreads until there is dissention. I am a peacemaker
at heart. When troubles come I want to run away. My husband
however was always ready to address any problem. He was
quick to tell you that God's house is not a place for confusion.
He believed everything should be done in decency and order.

There were by-laws for the church, and they were to be followed. If you did not adhere, you could leave. He did not beat around the bush about church discipline.

The difficulties that a pastor experiences from day to day are endless. There are people who get upset if the preacher fails to shake their hand. Then there are members whom the pastor forgot to visit. God forbid, he did not even know they were sick. Billy's pet peeve was people who thought they owned their pew. One lady asked guests to move because they were in her seat.

Happier Memories

There were some funny experiences. It was not all negative. In the 1960 era there was a T.V. program called "Rawhide". It was a western series that featured cattle drives. One of the famous lines in it was "Head em' up and move em' out. One Sunday morning as the ushers came down for the offertory a little lad in the back stood up on the pew and yelled, "Head em' up and move em' out!" I don't know what the offering was that day, but it sure brought a lot of laughter.

Our Sunday morning service was broadcast on the local radio station WFIV. One of the most embarrassing moments for Billy was losing his false teeth. He was preaching full force when suddenly his teeth flew out of his mouth. He was able to catch them before they fell on the floor, but the crowd went wild. Later people who were at home listening wanted to know what caused all the laughter.

There were more good times than bad, and I like to remember the good. The hair styles in those days were high and stiff. Wiglets were hair pieces that pinned on top to add prominence. During the service one of the parishioners with her three year old suddenly stood and rushed out. The curious little boy had pulled out her wiglet. Embarrassed, she carried the wig in one hand the child in the other.

My mother was the church pianist, and I played the organ. One Sunday the organ started making a sound like a motorcycle. Suddenly there was a loud boom, and the organ died. Of course the sound was heard on the radio. In an effort to explain, Billy told the audience that we would probably need to purchase a new organ. A memory I will never forget was a crippled man in our neighborhood who appeared at our door the next morning. He had been listening to the broadcast and wanted to give $500.00 toward a new organ. God had led him to help us, but the lesson he gave us was far greater. The old saying, "little is much when God is in it" is so true. Our hearts were blessed by his generosity. His worldly goods were few. He was crippled and could not walk, made leather goods and sold them for living expenses. Yet, he gave! It reminded me of the widows' mite. She gave all she had, and God blessed her.

Mark 12:42

And there came a certain poor widow, and she threw in two mites, which make a farthing. And he called unto him his disciples, and saith unto them. Verily I say unto you, more in, than all they which have cast into the treasury: For all they did cast in of their abundance: but she of her want did cast in all that she had, even all her living

My grandmother also played the church organ in her younger days. It was the old time pump organ that operated with the foot pedals pumping the sound. I did not have the privilege of seeing her play but was told she did well. I did enjoy hearing her play the harmonica. In the evenings she would go to the fireplace mantle where she kept the harmonica. We knew there was a treat in store and would dance around her while she played. She was proficient in her skills and played with little effort.

The church quartet often visited other churches and performed. They would ask Granny to play the harmonica. One night an older man with instrument in hand, proceeded to give a long dissertation about the difficulties and breathing techniques required for playing the harmonica. He struggled through one song. Later that evening, Granny, at eighty five years young put him to shame.

Many blessings came from ministry to others. One that I enjoyed was helping new mothers with their babies. I was called upon to help a mother who felt insecure with her first baby. Since I had birthed four little girls, I felt quite confident. However, I had never taken care of a baby boy. I arrived early to help give the first bath. Since he had been circumcised there were precautions. After the bath there was Vaseline applied to the circumcision and alcohol for the umbilical cord. How could I have confused the two? Yes, I used alcohol for the circumcision! Yes, the baby cried, and cried and cried. I felt so.......bad for the mom and the baby. She didn't call me for the next baby.

The holidays were all special. I loved Christmas the best. Hours of play practice and choir rehearsals culminated in the final production. My mom was a great coach for me. She told me in her later years that her desire as a girl was to become a teacher and marry a preacher. Ironically, my brother was a math teacher and I married the preacher. Mama loved the Christmas plays and helped me direct them. The costumes were made by hand and we kept them from year to year. My dad always made the cradle for baby Jesus and framed up the manger. It was decorated with the plentiful palmetto fronds found in the back pasture. After the Christmas program there was fellowship in the kitchen with cookies, cake and punch.

On Halloween, we always dressed up for a party on the creek bank. We had a greased pig race and a greased pole to climb. The one who caught the pig got to take it home. We had trails in the woods that held unforeseen mysteries in their path. One was a tape recording of a train whistle coming down the track. A huge spotlight was positioned in a tree to shine down on those few who dared to walk the trail after dark. Coming up out of the creek was a creature from the "Black Lagoon". Actually, it was the lead singer in our church quartet. He did manage to fool a few of us. One year Billy and I dressed as the rooster and the hen. I made chicken costumes that were quite amusing. Billy barked orders and I "cluck-clucked".

New Years Eve was celebrated in church from 7:30 till midnight with preaching, praying, testimonies and rejoicing. Local churches joined us to welcome in the New Year. Refreshments were always served afterwards. Baptist can't meet unless they eat!

Easter brought about the remembrance of the great sacrifice our Savior paid for our redemption. Spring bouquets decorated the church foyer and often palms surrounding the pulpit area. When I was twelve years old I gave my heart to Jesus. I was baptized on the following Easter Sunday. Easter was a special time for me. Not only did I celebrate the resurrected Christ but the second birth and baptism of my own life.

On Easter Sunday we put on our best clothing. In those days that meant hat, gloves, and a new dress. When the girls were little I loved dressing them alike. I made most of their clothes. Smocking was a technique my mother taught me. I loved to smock their dresses and spent hours perfecting them.

As I sit alone now in my senior years, I long for days of yesteryear. I loved caring for my precious girls and husband. I feel so blessed to have been able to be a homemaker when they were young. Billy never wanted me to work a secular job. He thought the woman's place was in the home and that was exactly where I wanted to be.

Billy was often away from home when he was called for revivals or church conferences. The girls always looked forward to daddy coming home. He always brought them back a new dress. He loved buying for them and had excellent taste in clothes. Ironically, he and I both were chosen "best dressed" for our senior class year books. I loved it when he took me shopping. He would wait outside the dressing room while I changed clothes. Then I would come out before him for approval. He always stated his opinion, good or bad! My favorite dress was a formal gown that he chose for me to wear to his college alumni dinner. When I came out of that dressing room and stood on a platform before three mirrors, I felt so blessed to have a husband that really cared.

CHAPTER IX

Major Move

The year of 1976 brought about major changes in our lives. We lived in my home town for the first eighteen years of our marriage. We lived next door to my mom and dad. We had the ideal family setting. The church was growing and there was the possibility of starting a Christian School. Billy had mixed emotions about venturing into this big undertaking. It had been decided to build a parsonage on the property with the church. We were living about thirty minutes away in the home we purchased in 1962. Some of the members felt the pastor should live closer. Plans were underway to build the house when Billy approached me one Sunday morning. He said, "Honey, I feel that God wants me to resign. I did not even take time to pray but replied, "Oh no, you just need to hire someone to help you". I was dead wrong and will never forget it. I started praying about it. One night I asked God to reveal through scripture what we should do. When I opened the word, the scripture I received was the prayer of Hezekiah. A prophet had prophesied his death. Hezekiah prayed God would extend his life and God answered, "I have seen your tears and heard your prayers. I will answer them". God extended his life. God heard my prayers as well and extended our stay. However it was to my sorrow. My selfish prayer was answered. Little did I know the heartache it would bring.

We began to experience extreme persecution from church members. There were multitudes of problems coming to us which eventually led to our leaving. The matter was put to a vote, but the result was not with what Billy felt comfortable to stay.

Never underestimate the power of Satan to discourage and humiliate. The year of 1976 was without a doubt the hardest year of our marriage. We moved out of our house and put it up for sale. We sold it to friends and watched them move in our beloved home of 15 years. I walked through the empty house one final time and recalled in my mind the good times. We moved in when Kathy was a baby and now she was in high school. I walked into a newly renovated kitchen and was reminded how our gracious God had provided several years earlier.

We had a neighbor who was a friend of my dad. She was elderly and had trouble getting around. I befriended her and often took the children over to see her. She was very lonely and loved visiting. I was able to share the gospel with her. She told me one day that she had a letter for me. She asked me to keep it until her death. Several years later she passed. When I opened the letter it was her last will and testament. She had left to me her savings. It was enough to remodel our Florida room into a kitchen. God works in mysterious ways. I never dreamed a visit to a lonely lady would result in blessings untold.

CHAPTER X

Gant Lake Baptist Church

Billy resigned the church in August of 1976. He received a call in October from the Gant Lake Baptist Church in Webster, Florida. They wanted him to preach in view of a call to pastor. The church was located in a farming community. The pace was much slower than what we were accustomed. We enjoyed the ride to the country, beautiful farm lands, cattle, hills and large oak trees.

We arrived early Sunday morning. Billy preached that morning and left nothing unsaid. He wanted them to know where he stood and what he believed. It was "take me like I am because I am not changing." That afternoon a group of deacons met with him to discuss the possibility of his taking the church. He told us later that he told them he needed $125.00 a week salary and 100 percent call. When he said 100 percent majority vote, one of the fellows who had been very quiet, spit on the ground and said, "Hell! You will never get it!" That night the church voted, and we were elected by 100 percent majority vote. God never fails! He can move mountains (and people)!

Jeremiah 32:17
Ah, Lord God! Behold, thou hast made the heaven
and the earth by thy great power and outstretched arm,
and there is nothing too hard for thee;

Billy accepted the call, and we began a new venture. Webster was a farming community. The biggest activity was the Monday Flea Market. The only day of the week that traffic was a problem. People came from all over the state for the antiques, hand crafts, vegetables, and multitudes of flea market items. There were several packing houses for produce. There was also a Cattle market on Tuesdays.

The church had a parsonage next door to the auditorium. It was convenient on Sundays to sleep an extra hour. We had always driven 30 minutes or more to our former church. The house was a white brick, four bedrooms with two baths. It was comfortable and our three girls for the first time had their own rooms.

The Gant Lake Baptist Church was located in the rolling hills of Sumter County. There were two oak trees in front of the building. A wooden bench was placed between them. The old timers often sat outside until preaching started. Some of them chewed tobacco while others smoked. "The bench has been there for years and it would be dangerous to mention removal," we were told.

The congregation included local farmers, ranchers, school teachers, a county commissioner and retired folk. They welcomed us into the fold with grocery showers. The offerings were not large, but the groceries compensated the monetary loss. When school started the Carlton family provided clothes for the girls. Bro. Hayes and his wife brought us beef for our freezer. Bro. Herring and wife provided vegetables of every kind and color. We did not lack for any necessity due to the generosity of these wonderful people.

The love shown to us by these people helped build back our confidence and endeared us to them forever.

AnaRae entered first grade at Webster Elementary. Putting my baby girl in school in a strange place was difficult. She cried and I cried day after day. However, it was not long until my little chatter box made many friends and the crying ceased. One of her favorites was Monica. She and Monica would re-enact commercials from the television. One was a car dealership. AnaRae would get on her hands and knees while Monica stood on her back and yelled, "I want to sell you a car!" They were great entertainment on a Saturday afternoon.

Lisa and Kathy both entered a new high school. They were blessed to meet Ms. Foster, Guidance Counselor. Hannah welcomed them and helped to make their stay at South Sumter High memorable.

Our neighbors were the Turner family. They took us in as though we were part of their family. Many happy days with Mama and Papa Turner, Jerry, Jimmy, Barbara, Lisa and Shirley were spent around the table swapping stories. Mama Turner was an excellent cook (especially coconut pie). Billy made the mistake one Sunday of bragging on Mama Turner's pie. The next month we received pies from every lady in the church to assure their pie would receive accolades from the pulpit. Billy was no dummy!

Since our income was low, Lisa and Kathy decided to seek jobs. Kathy found work at the local chicken farm. The money wasn't great, but she enjoyed singing to the chickens as she picked up their eggs. This was the first time the girls had ever experienced country life.

Lisa picked up a secretarial job in the County Courthouse. She was happy to have her own money to spend.

The first year my days were spent in loneliness. My parents had always lived near, they were gone. My friends that I loved, they were gone. I experienced day after day in tears. I had been hurt deeply and I lost the song in my heart. Billy said to me one day, 'Jean, you have hung your harp in the willow tree, you never sing anymore." He was referring to the scripture:

Psalms 139:1, 2
By the rivers of Babylon, there we sat down, yea, we
wept, when we remembered Zion.
We hanged our harps upon the willows in the midst
thereof.

He was right. Months passed before healing began.

God has a way of mending hearts and it usually involves people. Our dear friends Lance and Carol visited. God restored my joy through their encouragement and I did sing again.

God does turn sorrow into joy, although I would never want to experience again the hurt that we endured. I can say that it was the only way I could taste the grief that Jesus endured for me. He was the Son of God yet He was blasphemed, ridiculed and spat upon. What I experienced was only a drop compared to His suffering. It has made me eternally grateful for my Savior who died for me.

Isaiah 53:6, 7
All we like sheep have gone astray: we have turned
everyone to his own way: and the Lord hath laid on
him the iniquity of us all.

**He was oppressed, and he was afflicted, yet he
opened not his mouth: he is brought as a lamb to the
slaughter, and as a sheep before her shearers is dumb,
so he openeth not his mouth.**

The church had little money to hire a janitor. We placed
a sign-up list in the foyer for people who would like to
volunteer with the church cleaning. Most of the time they
were consistent; however, people tend to forget obligations
they dislike. Cleaning the church was not a popular job.

Since we lived next door to the church it was obvious
by noon on Saturday that someone had forgotten. Of course,
the pastor and family were responsible. I remember so well
one Saturday when "someone" forgot! I was sweeping the
sidewalk with furious strokes back and forth. Grumbling
under my breath I said to God, "Why do WE have to do the
dirty work?" It was as if God stopped me in my tracks; I
looked up and in my mind I got a glimpse of my Grandmother.
She was walking down an old dirt road to the church house
with a broom, mop and pail in her hands. She was whistling
a little song. Many times as a child I had gone down that
road with her. She loved her church. She had prayed God
would put one in her community. She was happy to clean the
church!! She wanted to clean the church!! And God said to
me, "Jean, you prayed to be like Granny. Are you not willing
to clean my church? I never complained again about cleaning
the church.

Many joyful days were spent in the six years we
ministered in Sumter, County. We loved the large oak tree
in the front yard of the parsonage. In the fall we raked piles
of leaves. The girls loved to play in them. At times we made

bon fires and roasted marsh-mellows. These were some of the greatest times shared by our family.

One of our deacons raised peanuts. He invited everyone to come over and enjoy boiled peanuts. He cooked them in a huge iron pot in his back yard. Sometimes he made "chicken per Lou" in his big black pot. There were no problems getting people to attend.

I loved driving through the country side. Fields of pepper, corn, watermelon and a variety of greens were seen for miles. Billy gained the confidence of the people by his friendliness and willingness to out in the field with them. He was never afraid of getting his hands dirty. He was brought up in a family of share croppers in North Alabama. He actually enjoyed getting out in the fields and back to his roots.

The church was growing and Billy always preached: "Ye have not, because ye ask not". He felt that being idle was not scriptural and so he again…began to build. The entire auditorium was enlarged and refurbished. During this time many of the old timers had given plastic flowers that were everywhere. An entire room housed old flower arrangements, tables and etc. which were not being used. He announced one Sunday morning that anyone who had claim to anything in that room could come and pick it up or it would be thrown away. That was a big mistake!

The church had a beautiful new sanctuary with a brick front and white columns. The inside had new red pews on red/black carpet. Billy believed there was only one color for a church's interior and that was red. The exterior was either red brick or painted white.

Recently I found a clipping that Billy would have loved:

Red is the color of sin and shame,
A stain on the hearts of everyone.
But red is also the color of power
And of sacrifice
It is the color of blood that
Cleanses and heals
And red is the color of love.

A nursery was added to accommodate the precious little ones God had given to our congregation. A group of young ladies established a choral group, The Gant Lake Chorale. The group sang for church on Sundays. They often traveled and sang for civic events and local churches as far away as Tallahassee, Florida. Lisa and Kathy were both involved in this ministry.

Bro. Dave, senior parishioner often, teased Lisa that his son would soon be coming home soon and he wanted them to meet. When he received his next three day pass, Mike headed home. Mike was tall and thin and handsome. Dressed in his military attire they were introduced and the rest is history.

Lisa graduated high school in 1978. She and Mike began their courtship singing together. Mike had an amazing tenor voice which captured her heart. Their voices blended together as if they had been brother and sister. Mike's mother Ozella played piano for them. The big secret that she and I kept for months was revealed in the months that followed. We both knew from the start God had put them together.

February 3, 1979 they were joined together in Holy Matrimony. The bridesmaids wore white gowns with fur trimmed jackets. They carried long stemmed red roses. It was a real "snow ball" wedding with the groomsman all in white tuxedos with red boutonnieres. The church was packed that Saturday afternoon with friends and family. Lisa and Mike sang to each other during the ceremony. It was a beautiful and sacred service.

Lisa and Michael Whitman
Snowball Wedding

After the wedding our friends, Barbara and Joe, held a fabulous reception for them. When they left for the honeymoon their car was filled with balloons. There were so many balloons that they failed to see their friends Bret and Jerry in the back seat. They stayed quietly hidden as far as Wildwood before giving the "big surprise" away.

Lisa and Mike will soon celebrate 36 years together. What a joy they have been to their parents. They blessed us with two awesome grandsons.

Kathy eventually graduated from the chicken farm to an office. She worked as a secretary after school and on Saturdays. One of my favorite stories was during Kathy's cheer leading years. She loved being on the squad and put her all into cheering. When her dad asked her to pray for our evening meal, she often would start the prayer as if she were cheering.

Billy was always strict with the boys that came courting. One evening Kathy had a date with a boy we had not met. Billy insisted that he come in to meet us. Jimmy came to the door wearing flip-flops. When daddy (who was an authority on proper dress) questioned him, "Son, do you not have a pair of shoes?" Kathy hid behind the door squirming with embarrassment. "I would be happy to buy you a pair", the preacher continued. The young man from a prominent family in the community did not know what to say.

Kathy dated this young man until he stuck his car in the ditch one night. It was late and Kathy did not want to call her dad. Instead, she called her friend Jerry to come and pull them out of their dilemma. All ended when her date discovered Kathy had another "boy" friend.

Lisa and Kathy were blessed during their dating years to have a little sister. AnaRae and her friend Monica liked to hide behind the sofa when the girls came in with their date.

One of the boys, Frank, had a favorite line he used on her, "Girl, why don't you go play in the traffic?" It would make her so furious that she would leave them alone.

Many happy days were spent at the Gant Lake Baptist Church. One of my favorite times was "Old Fashion Day." Everyone would dress in costumes of years gone by. The preacher read excerpts from sermons preached decades ago. My favorite was E.E. Gillentine's message on "Bobbed Hair and Sassy Women." Dinner was served under the oak trees on long tables. Women in their long dresses with bonnets, men in overalls, portrayed scenes from the pioneer days.

In July of 1979, I received a call from my brother that our mother had experienced a major stroke. She had been diagnosed with carotid artery disease and would need surgery soon. On my way to mother's room, before the surgery, I walked by the hospital gift shop. A bouquet of red roses on the top shelf caught my attention. I walked past the shop and stopped to see how much money was in my purse. My mother deserved those flowers, without a doubt. If ever there was a saint, it was my mother. She endured in her life time far more sorrow than joy. She was the one who put up with me, answered all my questions, dried my tears, and held my hand until I went to sleep at night. If it took my last penny, she was going to have them. It did! Ironically, they were the last flowers she received this side of the grave.

Her hug meant everything to me that day. "Take care of your daddy," she said as the stretcher carried her away. I am convinced that she knew she knew she was not coming back. The next ten days were agonizing. A cerebral hemorrhage occurred in the recovery room. She was declared brain dead and kept alive by machines. I stayed with daddy and we drove to Orlando daily to let her know we loved and cared for her, but she never responded. It was one of the most heart wrenching experiences of my life. Mama died seven days before daddy's 79th birthday. She was 67 years old.

As God has our ordained time before birth, we accepted the fact that He knew best. It was one of the saddest times of my life. On the way home from the hospital that evening, I remember thinking: "Now I am the mother! Granny is gone, mother is gone and I am left with no one." My precious Kathy drove me home that night. When I expressed my thoughts to her, she said, "Mama, I will be here for you, I will help you." That memory has never left me.

CHAPTER XI

Life's Challenges

Life went on that year. Christmas was the hardest. Billy built a house in Leesburg with a contractor friend. It was on Picciola Island. They had planned to build it for a "spec" house and sell it. When my spirits were so low, Billy decided it would help if we moved into the house. Perhaps new scenery would improve my depression.

It was fun living on an island. The shape of it was similar to the state of Florida. We were down on the point near the water. Our friends "the Mutters" lived near us. We took walks around the island in the evening. David had a boat and we sometimes would take boat rides through the canal and out in the lake. David loved to wait until just about dusk. He had a loud air horn on the boat. When all the little birds around the lake had just settled in for the night, David would blow the horn and birds would be soaring into the heavens. It was fun then but now I feel a bit guilty, poor birds!

While living on the island I spent much time praying. It was quiet and peaceful there. The girls were in school and I was alone most of the day. I remember asking God for a lot of things that year but one prayer remains clear. Billy and I had been in Alabama for a Revival meeting. The pastor's wife was a dear saint of God. She and I talked a lot and she told me things that God had done for her. A story I remember so well was how God showed her things through dreams. She said that each time her husband was going to be moved to a new field of ministry that God would show her in a dream where they would be going. I pondered much over this story.

So.........during this time of uncertainty in my life I decided to ask God. And I said, "God if you would show Sister Lowe where her husband is going next....Would you show me where we are going from here?"

As clear as it was yesterday, I remember dreaming that night of the lakefront in St. Cloud, Florida. Many times as a child I had been there swimming. There was a familiar water tower in the distance. When I woke up the next morning, I dismissed the dream as just that. Of course that wasn't God showing you anything. How could you think that? After all who are you to ask God to show you something? Dreams are just dreams??? Or are they?

In 1978 just one year before my mother's passing, she had emergency carotid artery surgery. While she was recuperating after the surgery she came over to stay with me. Mama told me that while she was in recovery she felt herself drifting toward a bright light leading to heaven. She said that she saw her mother, her cousin and a baby. As her mother reached to hand the baby to her she said to them, "No, it's not my time." She then felt herself drifting back on her bed. A near death experience? A dream? I don't know, only God does, but I do not doubt the truthfulness of my mother and her experience.

Mother and Daddy often spent week-ends with us. They missed the girls and of course it was a joy to have them. When Mother died in 1979 her funeral service was held in Gant Lake. She had become a part of the church family there and they loved her. Her body was laid to rest at Rose

Hill Cemetery in Kissimmee where her baby boy "Jerry" was buried.

The cemetery plot was purchased by my Great Grandfather Frank Bass. He brought his family to Kissimmee in the late 1800's from Americus, Georgia. My father Harold lived with his Grandfather Frank and "Other Mama" Emma Ada Tatum Bass. A huge lot with a tall marble monument signifying the Bass linage still stands today. Grandpa Bass, a building contractor poured concrete slabs over each of the graves. My father continued the tradition until his death. Each grave holds the unique handprints of my dad and his grandfather. I am so blessed to have the family history and the memories to share.

The cemetery lot holds the bodies of Needham Franklin Bass and his wife Emma Ada Tatum Bass and their beloved three children. Rosa Myra Montiel Bass and her husband John Woodall with four of their children and descendants are also laid to rest.

Mother's death left a huge vacancy in our family. She was our rock, the one to go to in the time of trouble. She was our prayer partner and was able to answer most of our questions. Mother's cooking ability far out- weighed anyone else in the family. Being the oldest in a family of five children, mother was accountable for cooking, cleaning and etc. She fed more preachers, missionaries and family members than I could ever count. Her life was one of service and her spirit was mercy and humility. I loved my mother and long for the day that God will unite us again.

We moved to Leesburg soon after mother died. Planning and organizing a new house occupied my mind. It helped to have dear friends who lived near and were of a great comfort to me at this time.

One of my favorite memories was a dinner that Frances and I planned to surprise our hard working husbands. To help our finances, Billy was working a part time job with David building houses. They often talked about how much they enjoyed going to the local restaurant for donuts and coffee in the mornings. They talked about the pretty waitresses and their red lipstick. Frances and I decided to dress as waitresses, wear bright red lipstick and invite them over after work. We prepared a new recipe called Volcano Salad. Veggies, meats, lettuce, cheese was piled onto a huge taco topped off with avocado. It did resemble a volcano. We sat them down and waited on them including kisses on the cheek. We heard little about the donut house after that evening. They took the hint!

Christmas came and went that year. Mother had always prepared Christmas dinner. It was not Christmas without her. Billy was working two jobs to keep up the payments on the house. It was my 40th birthday two days before Christmas. When the day came and went with no Happy Birthday and NO PRESENT, I broke into tears at bedtime. In the 21 years we had been married, he had never forgotten my birthday. He felt so bad and told me that I could open my Christmas present that was under the tree. Of course, I wasn't going to do that.....Spoil my Christmas? That was the last time he ever forgot my birthday!

On Sunday my dear friend Frances bought me a huge cake and shared it with the church congregation after services.

The following year 1980 we decided to move back to the parsonage and put the house up for sale. I had gotten a secretarial job at an Electronics plant in Bushnell. The two oldest girls were working in the same town. We thought the house would sell and financially it would be a burden lifted.

In March of 1980 our year changed, our family changed. We were blessed with our first grandchild......A BOY! It was the most exciting time. Some of the young people from church gave us a grandparent's shower! Gifts were a Brag book photo album, T-shirts that read Best Grandpa and Foxy Grandma, a car tag "I love my grandson" and many more hilarious presents.

Michael Aaron Whitman was born on March 20th. The arrival of his birth brought great joy into my heart. It helped to heal the deep hurt within me. Billy and I were at the hospital in the cafeteria when the news came that it was a boy! I had a coke in one hand and peanuts in the other. I became so excited that the drink and the peanuts went flying out of my hand onto the floor. We have a baby, a little one to love and cuddle, a boy!!!

I was so happy that we had moved back into the parsonage. Lisa and Mike only lived ½ mile from us. I spent as much time as possible enjoying that precious baby boy. He was so adorable, big brown eyes that revealed potential for mischief. We had a swing on the front porch of the parsonage. I loved to swing him and show him the moo cows in the pasture next door. His granny taught him to say MOO........... cows.

When Aaron was just a few weeks old, I stayed with Lisa to help her. Aaron had trouble with choking and we decided to take him to Dr. Carlson, the pediatrician. Being the thoughtful person I am, I took charge. Wanting to help Lisa, I carried the baby in the office and proceeded to tell the doctor his problem. He patiently listened to me and then said:

Let me speak to the baby's mother, addressing Lisa. He asked her some questions and then said, the mother is the care taker of the baby, the grandmother is to help with the chores.

Well, I went home that day and never really cared to go back to Dr. Carlson's office again.

When I had my children, I lived close to my mother and grandmother. They gave me advice and I took it. I figured if they had raised seven children they surely knew how it was done. If they told me to give them paregoric, then I bought paregoric. If they told me to give them an enema then I did what they said. NOT LISA….. If Dr. Carlson didn't say it then she didn't do it. Whatever Dr. Carlson said was law and gospel so mama just kept quiet.

In spite of my non effective efforts, Aaron survived and was the cutest little boy ever and the apple of his granny's eyes. I made his first little robe and printed on the back "granny's boy". Papa and I would argue over whose boy he was, He would say, "I'm papa's boy" and then just laugh when I contended, "No, he's granny's boy". Those were wonderful joyful days and then…..

CHAPTER XII

New Year

On New Year's Eve of 1981 we attended a church service in Crystal River. Pastor Wiley Wooten had invited Billy to preach that evening. It was a beautiful service and in closing we were asked to join hands and pray. Commitments were made. I felt that God wanted me to improve my music. Playing the organ in church was a real joy to me. However, I never felt adequate. Billy always preached to give your very best to Jesus. I felt that my skills could be improved if I had additional lessons. On that night I resolved to locate a teacher.

The following week after praying, I opened the phone book and found Jones Music Company, Leesburg, Florida. They were offering piano and organ lessons. I called and made an appointment. That call led me to a woman named Glenda Wood. We later would become lifelong friends. On the first lesson she played for me, I cried. We felt a connection in our kindred spirits. It was proof to me that God guided me in the right direction.

Glenda and her family, John, Suzie, Sandy and Rachael started visiting our church. On occasion she would go with us to revivals and play piano for me to sing. She was an accomplished pianist and organist. It was a blessing to have her accompany as I performed. Her music gave me a desire to sing. Many of my lessons were spent just listening to her play.

In the spring of 1982 Billy was finishing up a room for a church study. After nailing the last nail in the paneling he came back to the parsonage. "Jean, I believe God is going to move us" he said to me with self-assurance. I knew not to question him. I did not say a word.

Within a months' time we received a call from a group of men from St. Cloud, Florida. Two of the men were people we knew so we were not surprised when they said they wanted to come up for a visit. They said to have the coffee pot on and they would bring the donuts. Their visit proved to be evidence that God was up to something.

The men were part of a group of about 18 people who wanted to start a mission in St. Cloud. Missionary Fred Robbins had agreed to meet and hold services with them until they secured a pastor. Billy was their first choice. They were meeting in the Women's Club on Massachusetts Avenue. Billy did not give an answer but told them he would pray. I did not want to go back to Osceola County and had said that many times over. The old proverb, never say never would come back to haunt me.

After months of praying Billy agreed to accept the challenge. Even after he accepted the call I wanted God to show me and (I am not from Missouri). My Grandmother often told me about "putting your fleece before the Lord". She was referring to Gideon when he wasn't sure God would save Israel by his hand as he had said.

Judges 6:36-40
And Gideon said unto God. If thou wilt save Israel
by mine hand, as thou hast said,
Behold, I will put a fleece of wool in the floor;

and if the dew be on the fleece only,
and it be dry upon all the earth beside,
then shall I know that thou wilt save Israel by mine
hand, as thou hast said
And it was so: for he rose up early on the morrow,
and thrust the fleece together,
and wringed the dew out of the fleece, a bowl full
of water.
And Gideon said unto God, Let not thine anger be
hot against me,
and I will speak but this once: let me prove, I pray
thee, but this once with the fleece;
let it now be dry only upon the fleece, and upon all
the ground let there be dew.
And God did so that night for it was dry upon the
fleece only, and there was dew on all the ground.

I guess I will always be one that has to be shown. As a child of God I am sure it depicts lack of faith. But in my case I want to be positive that I am in the will and way of God. Had God not shown me, I would have gone because my husband felt called. Included in my marital vows were the words from the book of Ruth.

Ruth 1:16
Wither thou goest, I will go; and where thou lodgest,
I will lodge:
Thy people shall be my people, and thy God my God;

Shortly before our return to Osceola County, Billy was asked to conduct a revival in Pine Castle, Florida. Brother

Glen, pastor, was a former Youth Director for us in Orange County. We had been friends for years and both he and Billy loved to fish. On the last day of the meeting Glen and his wife Patsy took us on a picnic and fishing trip. We were late getting to the spot. The worms we bought were barely wiggling. Glen says to Billy, "Preacher, I believe God really wants you to come back to Osceola County!" I voiced my opinion and said well God is going to have to show me! Afterwards it came to me that I should put out my fleece. I knew that it had to be something that only God could answer. So......in my heart I said to God, "God, if you want us back in Osceola County would you let us catch 10 fish today." Now I know that some preachers say you should not pray that way. However I knew that my granny had many prayers answered and if God would do it for her then He would do it for me. I am sure that I will have some doubters who read this and say, not so. But, that day we fished until noon without one single bite. We ate our sandwiches and started fishing again. Glen says to me, "Jean, you had better start praying because fish do not usually bite in the afternoon. Early morning and late evening are the best hours for biting. When I took the worm out of the basket, it was not even moving. It was July and the sun was beating down on us. I kept praying, God if you want us to come back to Osceola County please let me know without a shadow of a doubt. Before long, I caught a fish, then Glen, then Patsy, then Billy. Before we knew it there were ten fish on the string. We kept fishing but not another bite, not one single nibble was seen. Does God hear a "fleece prayer"? You keep your doubts to yourself but I am a Believer!

It was hard leaving Gant Lake Baptist Church. The people loved us, and we loved them. Souls were being saved and hearts drawn close to Jesus, but it was our time to go. On our last Sunday my heart was moved with compassion as the people tearfully said goodbye. I said in my heart to God, "Will we ever find another place where people love like this?" And God said to me, "Whatever you give up for me, I will repay fourfold." I never questioned again God moving us. God is true to His word! We were loved fourfold in a new venture that would last over 27 years.

CHAPTER XIII

Eastern Avenue Baptist Church

God's ways are the best. When we are patient and allow Him full control, He will work all things together for good.

Romans 8:28
And we know that all things work together for good
to them that love God,
To them who are the called according to his purpose.

Billy closed every letter he wrote to me with this scripture. It was his favorite verse and he lived by it.

The church was sponsored by the Campbell City Missionary Baptist Church. Gene Vickers, pastor was glad to have Billy back in Osceola County. He had attended our church long before he himself became a pastor. His church was small but they were willing to give us a hand and be our "Mother" church. Bro. Robbins had done an excellent job organizing the mission. The first Sunday of August 1982 was the beginning of an exciting venture.

The meeting place for our church was an old community building in down town St. Cloud. We had an organ and a piano for the worship service. There was a kitchen, two bathrooms along with a large room where we used folding chairs to seat our congregation. Sunday School was divided into three groups. The toddlers were taught in the kitchen, first and second graders had the hallway between the bathrooms. The older children were in a mobile van provided by church members. It was difficult not having a church building. But the Lord was with us and we knew for certain He had directed us to this place.

In January of 1983 my organ teacher from Leesburg and her family felt led to come and help us in the ministry. That move entitled me to free lessons every Sunday. Glenda took the job of pianist and continued over 27 years.

By 1984 we purchased land for a building. The property was the former St. Cloud high school football field. It was located on Eastern Avenue therefore the church changed their name from Community Baptist Church to Eastern Avenue Missionary Baptist. In August of 1984 we moved into a new sanctuary. It was an auditorium designed for future educational purposes with six Sunday school rooms, two bathrooms and a church study.

The church was blessed to have men who were from varied fields of occupation. Under the leadership of the pastor the men volunteered their services and completed the building within three months. Many came after their eight hour shifts and worked into the night. It was a sacrifice but no one complained. God created unity among the workers and when the church was completed they physically knew they had been a part of building a house for God.

There was much excitement on the Saturday before our first Sunday in the new building. Men and women gathered to clean and perform last minute details. Some electrical wire needed to be strung through the attic. The minister of music offered to be the guinea pig. The finishing touches were almost completed when the music minister fell through the attic right above the pulpit. Thank God he wasn't hurt, but he said he would have rather faced the good Lord than his preacher that day.

The three hundred seat auditorium was full on dedication Sunday. The people were glad when they said, "Let us go into the house of the Lord."

Psalm 42:4
For I had gone with the multitude,
I went with them to the house of God,
With the voice of joy and praise,
With a multitude that kept holy day.

The minister of music, Bro. Lance Carpenter, led the music (under the patched hole above the pulpit) with joy in his heart to the Lord Brother Fred Robbins, the missionary was honored that day for his part in starting of the church. The pastor rejoiced as Tommy and Jacque Morris, former Music Minister now living in Arkansas, surprised us with their attendance. Pastor Rick Adams preached the dedication sermon and the preacher beamed with joy and thanksgiving.

Revelation 7:12
Saying, Amen: Blessing, and glory,
And wisdom, and thanksgiving, and honor,
And power, and might, be unto our
God for ever and ever. Amen

The thrill of finally being able to worship in a house built to honor God is only known to those who have experienced the wait. There is something to be said about "waiting upon the Lord."

Lamentations 3:25
The Lord is good unto them that wait for him,
To the soul that seeketh Him.

CHAPTER XIV

New Addition to the Family

Church services were held on Sunday, morning and evening. Wednesday night was prayer meeting but always with a sermon. May 8th of 1984 fell on a Wednesday night. Billy was about mid-way through the message when the church phone rang. One of the deacons ran to the study to answer and quickly brought the phone to me. It was Lisa calling to say that she was on the way to the hospital. She had gone into labor with her second child. Of course, I couldn't wave my hands and cut my throat to get Billy's attention. It was agony waiting until he finished the sermon. I'm sure it was the longest one he ever preached!

After the service we drove the sixty miles to Leesburg. We arrived just in time to see our second grandson, Timothy Adam Whitman. Grandparents always think their grandchildren are beautiful or handsome. But.......I was so worried about Adam. He was not a pretty baby. He had a lot of black hair that stood straight up, his skin was pale and I thought, Lord what can we do for this child? Thankfully God heard my prayers and by the time he was a year old his black hair had turned blonde and his blue eyes twinkled when he smiled. He was adorable! And he could sing! By the time he was three we would put him on a box and let him sing in church.

Adam and Aaron were inseparable yet entirely different. Aaron loved outdoors, playing ball, riding bicycles while

Adam preferred inside games. They were typical brothers. They fought occasionally but they were always friends. Both of these boys in later years would have near death experiences. When Adam was about 6 weeks old, Lisa and Mike left Aaron with his grandmother, Ozella Whitman, while they came down to St. Cloud. She took him with her on a Sunday afternoon drive. Aaron, being the active little boy he was, tried to grab the steering wheel. She lost control of the car. Aaron was thrown out the window while she lay pinned beneath the steering wheel.

Though we do not know and perhaps never will, why God allows accidents, tragedy, and suffering to come into our lives; we do know that He will be with us, He never leaves us. As we stood over this little boy with a huge gash in his lip and forehead we prayed. We didn't ask God why but thanked Him that he and his grandmother survived. God provided a nurse that night to pray with us. He always arranges for a person to minister to us in the time of our need.

When our minister of music resigned to further his ministry in music, our son-in-law Michael agreed to take his place. He remains today after driving every week end 75 miles one way for over 25 years. Michael was God sent to our family and to our church. Employed with Lockheed Martin in Ocala he sacrifices to serve as a minister of music on week-ends.

A funny story that Lisa likes to tell was about one of their trips home. It was after Sunday night service. Adam was a baby and Aaron was four. Michael got sick on the way home and she had to drive. They had to stop several times due to Mike's illness. Adam started crying, so she tried to hold and nurse him while driving. She said it was the worst trip ever, Adam screaming, Michael vomiting and Aaron singing a lullaby to Adam from the back seat:

"Hush, be still as a mouse,

there's a baby at our house.

Not a dolly, not a toy,

But a bouncing Baby Boy."

It was a sacrifice for the entire family but what a blessing they were to the Eastern Avenue Baptist Church.

Aaron and Adam Whitman
First Grandchildren

CHAPTER XV

New Fellowship Hall

The church continued to grow. By 1986 we were ready to build again. A fellowship hall honoring Bro. Harold Tripp was completed with a kitchen, bathrooms and bedroom for overnight guests. The building again was constructed by the men of the church. Billy at that time spent many days purchasing supplies for the night crew and then worked until late in the evening. He loved to tell about one of our winter visitors, Bro. Melton. He would come by the church while Billy was working to see if he needed anything. If he was out of material, Bro. Melton would go into town and purchase it for him. There was always a person willing to lend a hand physically and financially.

The fellowship hall was completed in August. It was also the Pastor's 50th birthday. The girls and I decided to surprise him with a "This is Your Life" party. I wrote the story as best I could remember from his stories. Months prior we gathered pictures from his scrapbooks. Slides were made into pictures and copied to a projector. Then music for the back ground was selected while a narrator provided the story. It was a lot of work and hours of so much fun. One entire night was spent putting it all together with the help of our son-in-law Michael.

After the morning worship hour we held a dedication of the new building. Lunch was served in the beautiful new fellowship hall. The birthday surprise came that afternoon.

A television was slipped into the auditorium covered with a sheet. When the Pastor came in, it was unveiled and the story of his life was played. He was one surprised preacher that day.

Many happy times were spent in the new fellowship hall; parties for new brides, showers for babies and dinners for "Old Fashion Days". Baptists are known for their love of food and fellowship. The bad part of fellowship is the "clean-up" and most parishioners are out the door when the party is over. The preacher and I with our girls spent many a long night washing dishes after a "Sweet Heart" banquet. By the time we arrived home we were too tired to be sweet hearts. The best part was the decorating and planning. The laughter and joy that fellowships brought far out-weighed the late cleanup.

CHAPTER XVI

Life in the Old Home Place

When God moved us back to Osceola County, I believe He had a two-fold purpose. Primarily we were sent to start a church; secondarily we were to take care of my aged father. After mama died Daddy was very lonely. He was living in the old home place built in 1887. A huge two story house was over whelming for him to keep. We talked with daddy about taking the money we had gained from the sale of our house in Leesburg and remodeling his home. He was in agreement and so we began months of repairing, painting and cleaning.

Kathy and AnaRae were still at home and they were blessed to live in my old homestead. I loved the old house. There were so many memories for me, sliding down the banister with my little brother. The same steps I walked down in my "Going Away" suit after our reception; the same front porch where my brother and I walked the banister, and the swing where I courted and received my first kiss. It was fun being home again and a joy to take care of daddy. He was such a sweet and caring person who never complained.

The girls were both in their teens. Kathy had graduated and was working with the First National Bank in downtown Kissimmee. AnaRae was in Middle School and had to make new friends all over again. The things they did not like in our home was "no air conditioning", one bathroom, and zero dryer for clothes. They truly went back to life in the fifties. We did have a washer but it was outside under a shed. The clothes had to be hung on a line. When they were dating they hated for the boys to see laundry hanging. The only difference between their time and my time was: When I was a girl, almost everybody hung their clothes on a line.

Billy obtained a secular job with an electrical and air conditioning company as purchasing agent. It was difficult for him. He worked long hours and then did hospital visitation and other pastoral duties. I was able to get a part time job teaching piano lessons at a local Christian school. It was tough, those early stages of the church. There were days that I even questioned whether we had done the right thing. But the church continued to grow.

Six years passed quickly and in 1988 Billy found a piece of property east of St. Cloud. He had desired to have his own home since we sold our first one in Kissimmee. The majority of preachers in our Association lived in parsonages. We had experienced the joy of living under the careful eye of overzealous parishioners. We felt the embarrassment of telling the church we needed a new septic tank. It was not easy to hear whispers in the business meeting, "What happened to the old one, is it really necessary?"

Daddy knew we had bought the land for a home and realizing his age and limitations offered to sell his home and divide the money between me and my brother, Harold. This would enable us to build a house on the property. In February daddy came down with congestive heart failure. He recovered but had difficulty breathing. It was necessary for me to be near. I left my position at the school and took piano students into our home for lessons. Daddy enjoyed the kids coming and going and endured the lessons. He loved to joke and tease. He was still able to do some wood working. He made wooden puzzles and gave them to the children. I loved my daddy!

We sold the old home place. Billy knew enough about building to be a contractor. He laid the footer and poured the floor of our new home. Designed to his specifications, our friends Barbara and David Jones drew up the plans and helped with specifics in building codes etc. In late February of 1988 the house was near completion. It was a Saturday afternoon. AnaRae and Kathy took lunch to their dad working on the property. They left in the early afternoon. He was to follow shortly thereafter.

We were getting worried when he didn't arrive home by five o'clock. A phone call that you never want to hear came next. "Your husband is in the St. Cloud Hospital. The doctor has determined that he has had a coronary thrombosis and is critical." When we arrived at the hospital he was unresponsive and a pale gray in color. For three days he remained in ICU. The physician told me that he had given him medication to break up the clot that had caused his heart attack.

I remember feeling like a child again only lost and abandoned. How would I make it without him? He was my rock! I could not stand, not alone! Helpless and confused I cried out to God. One of our parishioners (Mrs. Guthrie) upon hearing the news came at exactly the right time and prayed with me. Her face is vivid in my memory. God will never leave you alone! He always sends just the right person at the right time. This lady prayed so fervently that you knew she had touched heaven.

Billy did recover from the heart attack and was able to help with the finishing touches on the house. In March the house was completed thanks to the men of our church who took days off their jobs to help.

James 5:16
The effectual fervent prayer of a righteous man availeth much.

Psalms 34:15, 17
The eyes of the Lord are upon the righteous,
and his ears are open unto their cry.
The righteous cry, and the Lord heareth, and
delivereth them out of all their troubles.

Happy to be in our new home we rejoiced together. We had bedrooms for Kathy, AnaRae, and Daddy. It was a blessing to be near the church. The drive to and from was much shorter. We were far enough out of town to enjoy the sight of flocks of quail running through the yard. Occasionally we saw deer in the early evening. Daddy, an avid hunter in his younger years loved the new surroundings. However there were days that I knew he missed the old house especially the swing and the front porch.

CHAPTER XVII

Year of Crisis

Nineteen eighty eight proved to be a year of more tears than joy. In August daddy developed a severe case of congestive heart failure. He was admitted to the hospital in Kissimmee and spent days in ICU. I was spending every day with him. Billy came up to be with us one day and was complaining about a pain in his side. I suggested he talk with the doctor when he came in to see daddy. When Dr. Menk talked to him, he said, "Son, I think you had better let me examine you". He took him into an adjacent room. After examination he called in a surgeon. It was determined that he had a ruptured diverticulum and surgery was imminent.

Kathy was working in Kissimmee at the bank and was able to come and help out in the evenings. AnaRae was in her first year of college. She helped in the afternoons. But it was tough having the two men you loved, both in critical condition. I remember the doctor calling me "Florence Nightingale" when he saw me running from ICU to PCU each day. Billy's surgery was long and difficult. He suffered greatly and recovery was slow. Both he and dad were in the hospital over a month. Finally Billy was allowed to come home. He was still weak and needed my care. I continued to visit daddy but couldn't stay long periods. One day the doctor said to me, "Jean, I think you need to consider putting your dad in rehab." The thought of daddy not coming home grieved me. He had become incontinent and was so weak he could not walk. After talking with the family, it was agreed that we should put him in a nursing home until he was able to walk.

I believe one of the hardest tasks God ever gave me was looking for a Nursing Home for my dad. I visited place after place. When I entered the doors and saw the condition of the people there, my heart ached. I could not find a place that I felt was right for daddy. Of course, I wanted to take care of him but physically I knew that I was not capable of lifting him and Billy was not able to help because of his surgery. It was a time that I hope I never have to face again, being pulled between two people that I loved so much. Many prayers led me one day to a brand new facility. When I walked through the doors there was a brick fireplace. A room filled with rocking chairs and comfortable sofas that seemed like home. I was greeted by the new caretakers who seemed to be very caring. This is it! My heart felt better!

It was decided that the ambulance would transport daddy to the new home. Dr. Menk thought it better for him and for me. When I came out for a visit, he said honey, this is the nicest place and they have good food too! It helped me to know that he would only have to stay until he was better. But, daddy didn't get better and died on October 31, 1988. My heart was broken but I remembered the day he had given his heart to Jesus. I remembered that he and I had been baptized on the same Easter Sunday. I knew that he and mama were reunited in heaven and I rejoiced.

Revelation 7:15, 16, 17
Therefore are they before the throne of God,
And serve him day and night in his temple:

And he that sitteth on the throne shall dwell among them.
They shall hunger no more,
Neither thirst anymore;
Neither shall the sun light on them, nor any heat.
For the Lamb which is in the midst of the throne shall feed them,
And shall lead them unto living fountains of waters:
And God shall wipe away all tears from their eyes.

Billy had always been able to have some type of secular income. Now his health was declining and it seemed best if I found a job. I began to pray about a place to work. I enjoyed secretarial jobs and had always had a love for the medical field. I asked God if He wanted me to go to work would he please bring the job to me. I know it sounds ridiculous and I was willing to make my resume known but, where? I answered a few local positions listed in the newspaper but to no avail. One day as I busied myself with house cleaning, the phone rang. When I answered the man asked to speak to Doris. When I told him Doris did not live here, he replied that he had a resume in hand with this phone number. So I said what kind of job did she apply for? A medical receptionist was the reply! "I have been looking for that kind of job," I tried not to sound too eager". Well, he said, "Bring me your resume!" I promptly dressed and went to the office of Pediatrician. When the doctor saw me in the waiting room, she asked the nurse, "Who is that lady?" The nurse replied, "She is applying for the receptionist position." "I want her," the doctor replied. She too had been praying and felt that God said, "She is the one!" God always answers on time! I got the job thanks to HIM!

Psalms 9:11

Sing praises to the Lord, which dwelleth in Zion:

Declare among the people His doings.

That job began a twelve year venture for me in the medical field. The job with the pediatrician proved to be a Godsend for my grandson Aaron. When Aaron was about six years old we noticed him acting out. He seemed to have a twitch in his eyes. Then we noticed he had repetitive hand and feet motions. I asked the doctor one day if she knew what might cause this problem. She immediately replied that she thought he should be tested for Tourette syndrome. When I shared this with Lisa and Michael, they took him to Tampa for observation by a Neurologist. Dr. Gunderman, a pediatric Neurologist began treatment and has been not only an excellent doctor but a friend to our precious grandchild.

Aaron suffered greatly in his elementary years from bullying. Children who did not understand the Tourette syndrome made fun of his involuntary movements. This would bring much heartbreak to his parents and grandparents. Dr. Gunderman tried different medications and finally found one that helped control his tics. This is a heartbreaking condition and many prayers have gone up for a cure.

My job with the pediatrician was enjoyable. The nurse and I became friends and we spent many hours together. Each day was something new and learning medical terminology was interesting.

Billy's health improved and by the year end of 1988 we felt like we were going to survive. The Lock Haven Baptist Church where we pastored for 18 ½ years invited us to their

"Homecoming." It was a service honoring former pastors and members. At the service they surprised us with a gift entitling us to a Cruise from Ft. Lauderdale, Florida to various ports in Mexico. It would be scheduled for January 1989.

CHAPTER XVIII

New Year

We were happy to see 1989 come in and glad to see the close of '88. The year looked promising. AnaRae would graduate with her AA degree in June. Kathy's career in banking was successful and she was getting married soon. She was introduced to a young man whose father was a preacher. Two P.K. (preacher's kids) had a lot in common. I thought Ray had the kindest eyes. That was a positive to me and if anything counts it sometimes is mom's approval.

Our cruise to Mexico was most enjoyable. Our dear friends, David and Frances Mutter joined us on the trip. We talked and laughed until our sides hurt. David known for his pranks was at his best. He was an extremely generous person; when the Mexican children would beg for money saying, "dollar, dollar." David handed them double. It was not long until we saw David with ten or more children following him.

Matthew 19:14
Jesus said, Suffer little children
and forbid them not,
to come unto me;
for of such is the kingdom of heaven.

David Mutter is one of the greatest personal examples of Jesus that I ever knew. Not only did his words speak but his actions were even louder. His love for people and especially for children far outweighs any that I have witnessed. He and his wife Frances were more like brother and sister to us. Their friendship endeared us to them forever.

Kathy and Ray Turman Wedding

March of 1989 brought the wedding of Kathy Ann Rigsby and Ernest Ray Turman. I consider it not a coincidence but an act of God that these two were put together. Kathy made a list of the things she wanted in a man before she met Ray. Ray met all of her criteria including "an adventurous man." Several years later when she was spooked, while hiking on the side of a mountain range, she regretted her statement.

I am reminded that my grandmother always said, "Be careful what you pray for! God may give it to you!"

Kathy was beautiful in her pale pink lace gown and bouquet of sweetheart roses. Our friend David stood in for Billy while he walked her down the aisle. The wedding was a precious time for us. To see our Kathy aglow with happiness and to know that she was uniting in marriage to one who loved her unconditionally, was to know our prayers had been answered.

It was comical to me but one day I happened to remember when I was pregnant with my children I always picked out names for boys. My name for each one was Michael Ray. Since we did not have a boy it was ironic to me that my son-in-laws turned out to be Michael and Ray. I think God has a way of answering our prayers in ways we can never imagine.

Kathy continued to succeed in her career and was transferred to First Florida Bank on Orange Avenue, business district, of Orlando. It was a big step for her from the small community bank in Kissimmee. She had some adjusting to do driving in the big city and the commute was thirty miles further. She loved her job and was extremely happy with her adventurous husband. We called him "Tom Selleck." Some years later that adventurous husband would take her further than she ever dreamed she would go.

In June of '87 our baby girl graduated from Osceola High School. Following in the footsteps of her mother and grandmother she walked the aisle and received her diploma from OHS. The graduating class would have their ceremony in the Tupperware auditorium near Kissimmee. Billy was asked to do the invocation for the service. AnaRae's friends showered around us and we loved this special moment for all of them.

In September AnaRae enrolled in Valencia Junior College, Orlando, Florida. She had a part time job as receptionist for a nail salon. This helped with her travel expenses. When she was sixteen she told her dad that she wanted a sports car. Now the difference between AnaRae,

Lisa and Kathy were varied. Lisa was content to drive whatever her dad chose for her. She did not complain and Kathy was likewise. But AnaRae being the different child that I prayed for, was "high maintenance." She said that we taught her to pray specifically for what we wanted. She wanted a sports car! Shortly afterwards, a little blue Mazda appeared in our neighborhood with a "For Sale" sign in the window. Billy investigated: The owner was a local fireman who needed to sell it quickly for cash. AnaRae's prayer was answered!

Lisa and Kathy were not happy campers but AnaRae was delighted. Her love for cars came from her dad. She followed him around from car lot to car lot when she was only four. She could tell you every make and model of vehicles we passed on a road trip.

Luke 11:9
And I say unto you,
Ask, and it shall be given you;
seek, and ye shall find:
knock, and it shall be opened unto you.

John 15:7
If ye abide in me,
and my words abide in you,
ye shall ask what you will,
and it shall be done unto you.

If there was one thing that we stressed to our children, it was the importance of prayer. Time after time we related to them our experiences to save them from making the same mistake. Life is not about what we want but what God wants for us.

AnaRae went on to finish her last two years of college in Tallahassee at Florida State University. What an exciting time for her. We loved going up to visit. Her degree in Education led her to an internship in Orlando, Florida at Oakridge High School. It was a challenge, but she loved teaching.

In the fall of 1992 AnaRae was introduced to Jeffrey Miller a cousin of her friend Natalia. We were familiar with the family as Billy had at one time worked with Jeff's grandfather. We were pleased when AnaRae came home and told us she had a date. She was so excited and wanted it to be perfect. She gave instructions to the family: "I want the fireplace to be burning! I want mama sitting on the couch sewing and daddy in his chair reading." Of course, we obliged. We were impressed with the handsome young man who appeared at the door. Billy had to share with him some of the experiences that he had with his grandfather Miller. We sent them off that night not realizing they would soon become inseparable.

When they announced their engagement in January, we were not surprised. They seemed to be made for each other. Plans began for a wedding in June.

CHAPTER XIX

New Experience

In the meantime my job with the pediatrician changed. I was given the opportunity to work in the hospital Imaging Department. This was a whole new world for me and one that would benefit me for what was ahead in my life. I started out transporting patients to and from x-ray and working in the file room. What a chore to pull those charts full of x-rays out and distribute them for each patient that arrived. It was a real education learning to work with doctors. Most were very kind but then a few were arrogant and intimidating. One in particular I disliked. It was soon learned that I was a preacher's wife. One of the doctors' teasingly called me "the church lady." I entered the Radiology office with a load of x-rays one day. This doctor says to me, "Church lady, you need to pray for this man" (the one I disliked). Without thinking I said, "I would but it would not do any good." That started "World War Three" with me and the doctor. The doctor who teased me loved it and went down the hall laughing his head off.

In spite of my clash with the physician, I was awarded employee of the month for my rapport with the patients. Our director, Tom, said I could charm the disgruntled patients into thinking they didn't have a problem at all. I was grateful for the compliment and knew that only God could have given me the patience to deal with all kinds of people. Plus, I did a lot of praying!

In a couple of years I became more competent at my job. I was promoted secretary to the new Radiology Director, my friend Carol. It was a joy working with Carol. We had much in common and spent many hours together. March 25th was Carol's birthday. I talked with some of the x-ray techs and we decided to surprise her. We bought a cake and candles that you could not blow out (they just kept burning). We picked a slow afternoon and decorated one of the exam rooms with birthday décor. We called Carol in and lit the candles. We did not realize that the hospital rooms were set up with sprinkler systems in case of a fire. The smoke from the candles caused the fire alarm to go off and the fire department came in and helped us celebrate. What FUN!

There was a young man that came to work for us as a transporter and file clerk. He was a good worker but seemed to have a chip on his shoulder. His attitude turned people away from him. He sometimes had a smart mouth and employees often shunned him. I believe God spoke to my heart to befriend him. I learned through years of experience and dealing with people that external brashness is sometimes a result of deep hurt. This proved to be the case with Mike. We usually ate in the hospital cafeteria. I happened to sit at his table. Over lunch that day he told me his story. Abused by an angry mother, he showed me scars where she had poured boiling hot water on him. He left home as a teen-ager and came to live with his brother. Nothing seemed to be going right for him. I talked to him that day about allowing the Lord Jesus into his life. He seemed receptive to my invitation for him to visit our church. One of my greatest joys was the day he walked the aisle and gave his heart to the Lord. Mike was faithful to attend church. The last time I saw him, he was married and had two adorable little girls. Many times I have used this illustration in teaching. Be kind to those who are hostile. There may be a deep hurt inside.

Titus 3:2
Speak evil of no one,
....be peaceable, gentle, showing all humility
To all men.

"Your witness is only as strong as your character". - (Our Daily Bread, Oct. 2014)

CHAPTER XX

The Wedding

Having the joy of three daughters also brought the joy of three weddings! The third and final purse draining! But what a pleasure to see those girls gracefully and glowing in their elegant gowns of white. Aside from the decisions of color and cost of flowers, cake and who is going to be a bridesmaid, there is the ceremony to be composed by the preacher. Billy was a nit-picker when it came to weddings. He wanted them to be a sacred ceremony that God would honor. He did not allow pictures to be made during the ceremony. He abhorred wedding coordinators that were bossy and obnoxious. There were times when he put them in their place if they got out of line and did not adhere to the "Emily Post" etiquette. I have saved the Wedding Planner by Emily Post that we used for our first wedding ceremony. It is tattered and worn but was used for 52 years and taken to every rehearsal. God bless that precious old book that got us out of many arguments.

One of the greatest family moments was picking the wedding dress. Having dad's approval of the dress was important. He delighted in helping choose plus he had exceptional taste. We loved watching each of the girls stand before us on pedestals. Their reflections created by giant mirrors made my heart skip a beat. I loved my girls, they are my flesh and blood with a little bit of their dad's genes. What greater joy is there than to bear children? But the ultimate is to watch them grow from tiny babies into mature adults. Observing them live their lives according to biblical principles. And seeing God bless each of them as they marry the man God chose for them.

Wedding of Anna Rae and Jeff

June 21, 1992 the wedding of AnaRae Rigsby and Jeffords Miller was performed. Billy assisted by Judge Miller, Jeff's dad, conducted the service. They stood under a lattice arch covered with crimson bougainvillea vines. Billy made the arch along with a gazebo that was placed in the reception room. It was also covered with the bougainvillea. Bridesmaids wore flowered off the shoulder tea length dresses. AnaRae's gown was fashioned similarly in white satin with ornate trim. The bride and groom were stunning! They said their goodbyes from a turquoise and white 1955 T-Bird borrowed from Jeff's dad's car collection.

The following year brought change in our family that we never expected to happen. Our Sundays continued to have all the children around the table. We were now blessed with three son-in-laws, Michael, Ray and Jeffrey. We had two grandsons Aaron and Adam. The children and their spouses all attended the Eastern Avenue Baptist Church. What a blessing it was to sit back and see all of your children serving God and sitting in the same pews every Sunday. But, that was about to change!

On Easter Sunday of 1993 Kathy and Ray loaded everything they had in two trucks. With the help of Ray's twin brother, Roy and my friend Madeline they pulled out for Elko, Nevada. Kathy's adventurous husband had taken a job with Barrick Gold Mines in the far west. I will never forget that day as long as I live! I thought my heart would break! It was so far from home, who would take care of them? What if she became ill? Why so far away? I wore constantly a gold bangle bracelet that Billy had given me. I took it off that day and gave it to her. Somehow I felt that would keep us close. It was so hard for me to give her up, but she had prayed for an adventurous man and that he was!

Our Only Grand Daughter
Mary Hannah Miller

The hardest thing in life for me was to trust God for my children. As a mother it is good if you can be there for them. Put a cloth on their head for headaches, a water bottle on their tummy for stomach aches but 10,000 miles away would make that impossible. Billy shared the hurt with me, he wept, I wept, the girls cried until we could cry no more.

This adventure to the far west was one that has lasted twenty three years.

August 21st of 1993 brought us our third grandchild! A grand-daughter!! Mary Hannah Miller, a brown eyed beauty! She was the apple of her Papa's eyes. She would become our princess! Papa could always find something to buy for her. He would go shopping with us only because he could push her in the stroller. People always admired her. She would smile and wave to draw attention.

In November when she was three months old, Kathy came home for a visit. All of the family came to the airport to meet her. Tears of joy streamed from our faces. I'm sure people thought somebody had died in our family. We had welcome home signs stained with our sniffles. It was overwhelming to me, just seeing her again. I thought my heart would beat out of my chest.

Mary Hannah Miller

Kathy fell in love with Mary Hannah. We enjoyed her visit and spent every minute asking her questions about her life in the west. Papa's concern was, "Did she find a church? Was she happy there?" What a blessing to learn that she had settled into a wonderful church. People who worshipped in the same manner she was accustomed. She was taking voice lessons and singing with the choir. Papa was satisfied!

The visit, of course, did not last long enough. We were sending her back with the same sorrow but a confidence that she was happy.

A new baby helped heal our sad hearts. Mary Hannah was adorable. When she was about three years old, Papa and I would take her out to eat on Friday nights. She loved macaroni and cheese at Olive Garden, then top it off with a slice of double chocolate cheese cake. We loved to buy her gifts. She was always grateful and we loved it when those big brown eyes twinkled with delight. It was like having AnaRae all over again.

It was so much fun to make little dresses again. Every Easter, Christmas and Birthday granny brought out the sewing machine.

Mary Hannah Cooking

Mary Hannah loved helping in the kitchen. Many days were spent letting her play with biscuit dough. She liked to cut out cookie dough with different shapes. A few days before Christmas, I invited her friends Nora and Jordan to come over and make a gingerbread house. After about four hours of crumbling gingerbread and icing spread from head to toe, Nora put both hands on her hip and announced: Ms. Jean, this is a disaster! It truly was and we never tried it again but the memory is priceless.

One morning she slipped in my room when I was dressing for the day. I heard her giggle and turned just in time to hear her say; Granny, you are a "fat little bunny." From then on that was her favorite name for me.

Papa baptized Mary Hannah, his only granddaughter. She grew up listening to his sermons. The poor child didn't have a chance to be bad. One grandfather was a Baptist preacher and the other a Circuit Judge. She walked a straight line, most of the time.

In a few weeks from the time of this writing she will graduate from the University of Florida. In November of 2015 she will be married to her high school sweetheart.

Her papa's favorite line for her was; Mary Hannah is my favorite granddaughter!

CHAPTER XXI

New Chapter/New Sanctuary

The church with its continued growth was considering expansion. Adjacent property was purchased and plans were designed for a new auditorium. Billy was thrilled with the thought of building. It would be a major project but he was ready. Blessed with contractors, electricians and plumbers the men again would put their talents together and construct the building. There were hours spent in preparation. The most difficult was dealing with the City of St. Cloud. The building department required one parking space per four people. The church would seat 700+ and we did not have adequate room for parking. After much prayer Billy was able to get approval from the Seventh Day Adventist who owned adjacent property to use their parking spaces on Sunday.

On Easter Sunday 1995 we dedicated the new sanctuary built by men who honored God with their talents. The people who labored unselfishly were the ones blessed with glowing countenances on that day. The red carpet with white pews with brown trim confirmed Billy's signature colors. Red for the blood of Jesus and white for the remission of sins, he said was scriptural.

I will never forget when we revamped our fellowship hall one year. He wanted red carpet as usual. I convinced him to allow the ladies to pick the carpet. Much to his dismay, they picked a blue/green color. When the carpet was laid it was found to be flawed. The carpet had to be replaced and guess what? He couldn't get the same blue but they had it in red! I never tried to argue color again! I figured he had more power with God than me.

The first wedding in our new church was Kay Shull and Bob Lingerfelt. Kay and Bob both lost their spouses due to illness. They met through a mutual friend and it was a perfect match. Both in their sixties they beamed with happiness during the ceremony. They would become lifelong friends to the two of us along with Russ and Wanda Royer. The six of us spent many evenings fellowshipping in Kay's kitchen.

The church is a body of baptized believers who are covenanted together to carry out the teachings of the Lord Jesus Christ. Churches are made up of people. People are human beings with human frailties. When God blesses, you can be sure Satan will show up to discourage. We never started a building program without contention from the enemy. This building was no different. Conflict appeared shortly before we moved in the new building. About ten families left the church to start their own. Their efforts and results were not materialized and the people were scattered. By this time in our ministry we had learned not to fret over those who leave. God puts together the body and sometimes he removes to make room for others. God has a way of using calamities to work out His purpose in the lives of His people.

The church continued to grow. The fall brought many folks escaping the winter's fury in the north east. We loved our northern friends. Many were from other denominations but they loved our southern hospitality. Billy loved it when they came out the door after morning service with: "You know, preacher, we don't do it this way up north!" His reply,

"Well sir, you're in the South now." They got the message, "when in Rome, do as Rome does."

Our crowds increased. We moved our nursery from the youth building to the auditorium. A dressing room used for brides was converted to a nursery for infants. Because of the crying infants, carpet was put on the walls as a sound board. This room proved to be a constant source of complaint for those who sat on the back row. You can never please the entire congregation. The mothers were happy to have their little ones in the same auditorium. The older folks were bothered by the noise. God bless all the pastors who listen to complaints day after day with a smile on their face. It is not surprising that many leave the ministry due to stress.

Once during our ministry at Lock Haven, I recall Billy coming out of his office with broken blood vessels in his forehead from hours of praying through a conflict. It reminded me of the scripture when Jesus prayed in the garden of Gethsemane.

Luke 22:44

And being in an agony he prayed more earnestly: and his sweat was as it were great drops of blood falling down to the ground.

If the body of Christ knew the suffering that many pastors experience, they would spend more time praying and less time grumbling. It is tough watching your husband spend days and nights ministering to others and then listen to the same people tear him down on business meeting night over some miniscule issue. However, over years of experience, you learn to accept constructive criticism. Many times it is for our good. Learning to discern the motives behind a critical spirit is an advantage.

Our best years in the ministry were spent at Eastern Avenue Baptist Church. We were blessed with people who had much love to give. They gave freely of their time, talents and income. When the mortgage on the church/property was paid in full, it was a big relief. To start with nothing, not even a church hymnal and end with three buildings and be totally debt free is proof that God was with us.

Billy began experiencing chest pain. After a nuclear med heart scan he was diagnosed with heart blockages. We were introduced to an amazing physician Dr. Barrett. Born in Texas and a real southern gentleman he and Billy had a connection. He remains a friend as well as physician to our family. A former Internal Medicine physician he also trained in Cardiology. In years to come he would treat Billy for major four way heart by-pass surgery, abdominal aneurysm, carotid arteries and two strokes.

After his recovery from open heart surgery the church gave us a trip to the mountains of north Georgia. The cabin, a two story, three bedroom was nestled at the base of the great Smoky Mountain range. Our friends Bobby and Sue Bright came down from Alabama. We toured village shops in the little mountain towns picking up souvenirs. We traveled to Helena and other places of interest within a day's drive. It was a relaxing time with lots of laughter.

CHAPTER XXII

Vacations and Grandchildren

One of my failings was not keeping a record of the weddings and funerals my husband conducted. Billy was well known in the community. His motto "Stand up, Speak up and Shut up" was appreciated by folks. His funerals were not long and drawn out. He managed to tell a brief account of the deceased personal life. Then he brought the plan of salvation into every funeral. He said it was the perfect time to reach people with the gospel. Only eternity will reveal the lives he touched.

Many plans our family made were altered due to funerals. We determined one summer to take Aaron and Adam to Nashville and visit Opryland. We were to visit family in North Alabama then proceed to the big city. We arrived in Guntersville, Alabama in time for Papa to buy some worms for fishing. We had reservations for a hotel located on the Tennessee River. The boys got out their fishing poles and baited them with the largest earth worms I had ever seen. They were having the time of their lives trying to see who would catch the biggest catfish. The worms were so big I assumed it would take a huge fish to even swallow one.

That evening Papa received a call from the church back home. Someone from our congregation died and the family requested that he conduct the funeral. Of course, he never said no. Not wanting to disappoint the boys, he decided to get a plane out of Birmingham and leave us in Guntersville at the hotel. Bro. Bobby Bright, preacher friend, agreed to watch over us. The only problem we experienced was: The first night Papa was gone; the boys left the lid off the box of giant worms. It was quite a sight seeing the three of us search our room from top to bottom. I could not dare to sleep with the thought of one worm loose in my bed.

Papa returned safely and we made our trip to Nashville. Opryland was in full swing at that time and the boys had a great time. One evening Papa announced to the boys, "I want you to get your baths and dress nicely. Papa is going to take you to the greatest place to eat in Nashville." The "Opryland Hotel" was an exclusive hotel with superb dining. The mammoth building with gardens of flowers blooming inside and out was breathtaking. A harpist playing the strings of a golden harp provided music for our evening. A spiral staircase adorned with vines of green led to the melodic sounds. It was definitely different from anything the boys had ever experienced.

They seated us in a booth in the dining area. A tall waiter dressed in black tuxedo with a table linen over his shoulder appeared. He addressed the boys with: "The children's menu has hot dogs or chicken fingers." Papa spoke up quickly, "Now boys, you do not have to order from the Kids menu. Get whatever you want tonight." Aaron, a bit timidly says, I think I'll have a T-bone. Adam quickly followed, I'll have the same!" Papa looked at me and said, "Do you want a hot dog or chicken fingers?"

We laughed many times over our vacation with our precious boys. They were good children and such a joy. We loved every minute spent with them.

Our first trip to visit Kathy and Ray in Nevada was planned for June. When we arrived they surprised us with a trip to Yellowstone for our 35th anniversary. What a grand experience, the beauty of America's first national park was breathtaking. A mountain wild land of wolves, elk, bison and grizzly bears plus the beauty of Old Faithful, geysers and other thermal features. An added feature on our venture was a beautiful snowfall on June 8th our anniversary.

This trip gave us confirmation that Ray and Kathy were happy living in the west. They loved the rugged mountain life. Their home in Nevada was surrounded by the majestic Ruby Mountains. Capped with snow almost year round it was an impressive sight.

Ray was working with Barrick Gold Mines a global industry that was thriving. Kathy obtained a position as administrative secretary to the CEO. She met many interesting people in this position including President George Bush, shareholder in the company. She loved her job which also included organizing parties, meeting and greeting the elite executives who visited.

That job abruptly ended in December of 1997 with the birth of our fourth grandchild. Born prematurely two days before my birthday Nathaniel Ray Turman burst into the arms of elated parents. Kathy's prayers were answered and her dreams fulfilled. After 9 years of waiting she promised God if He would give her a child, she would stay and home and do her best to raise him in the admonition of the Lord.

I Samuel 1:11

And she vowed a vow, and said, O Lord of hosts,
if thou wilt indeed look on the affliction of thine handmaid,
and remember me, and not forget thine handmaid,
but wilt give unto thine handmaid a man child,
then I will give him unto the Lord all the days of his life,

It was January before I was able to see this long anticipated little boy. Lisa and I braved the cold ice and snow. A winter storm came in as furious as a hurricane. Snow covered the porch and winds blew the screens off the windows. But it was warm and cozy in the little house nestled in the valley below those stately mountains. The rocking chair rolled and lullabies filled the air.

Hush be still as a mouse,
There's a baby at our house,
Not a dolly, not a toy,
But a bouncing baby boy.
Rock a bye baby up in a tree-top
When the wind blows the cradle will rock
When the bow breaks the cradle will fall,
And down will come baby, cradle and all.

Nathaniel Ray Turman
First Christmas

God had so wonderfully blessed this little family. The love bestowed upon this little boy could only be described as grandiose. To be born surrounded with such love could only end with a lovable child and that he became. However, he was a typical boy in his formative years. He loved ropes and string and climbing, then skate boards and golf and baseball.

Nate loved roasting marsh-mellows. When it was too cold to go outside, Kathy would let him roast them over a candle. One evening after being denied to roast them, Kathy sent him to his room. She did not realize that he carried the marsh-mellows to bed with him. The next morning she discovered he had tried to roast his marsh-mellows over a light bulb. There were melted, gooey, singed marsh mellows on the lampshade, floor, walls and bedspread.

Kathy taught Sunday School for the Spring Creek Baptist Church. She taught the three and four year olds and of course Nate was in her class. Kathy was so adamant about keeping her promise to God that Nate had to sit every morning at home and listen to a Bible story. She tried very hard to make this little boy into the perfect gentleman. In spite of her efforts he was a typical boy who loved guns. One Sunday her lesson was on Jesus calming the storm on the Sea of Galilee. She asked the question, "Do any of you get scared at night?" One little boy spoke up answering, "I get scared of monsters coming to get me". Kathy then asked the question, "Can anyone tell John what to do when he gets scared?" Immediately Nate goes over to John. Kathy's chest puffs up thinking, Nate is going to advise him with sound biblical advice that I've taught him. Instead Nate says to John, "If you will get your tommy-gun out from under the bed you can shoot those monsters dead!"

Papa loved to tell Nate stories and this one was the best yet. His sermons always managed to mention the grandchildren and grand they were.

Nate Praying in the Snow

CHAPTER XXIII

Employment Change

In 1998 I was offered a job as Front Office Supervisor with the Kissimmee Outpatient facility. It was another Imaging company near the hospital. It was a new adventure and quite unexpected. We had a great radiology group from Orlando Regional Hospital. The hardest part for me was trying to keep the office staff happy and dealing with changes in insurance. I did enjoy my new job with some great people who kept me busy.

Being a Supervisor and making pertinent decisions was new for me. It taught me many lessons. I have never succeeded in discerning people. Hiring new office personnel was difficult. Billy often remarked that I was a push over. He said people could talk me into almost anything. One difficult lesson for me was over an employee I hired. I thought she was a competent transcriptionist. After a few months of incompetency I placed her in another position. She was annoyed about the change and decided that she wanted my job. After several rumors started in the office I learned she was trying to get me fired. The job was stressful in itself and I certainly did not need the stress of a disgruntled employee. My only solution was to pray: Dear God, move me or move her, was my distressing cry. It is never too late to pray....A few weeks later, she informed me that her husband had gotten a job transfer and she was moving to Georgia. I wished her well and then thanked God he had blessed them with a new endeavor.

My grandmother taught me, it is better to pray than to fret. Most problems are resolved without anxiety when we allow God to handle them.

Philippians 4:6
Be careful (anxious) for nothing;
but in everything by prayer and supplication
with thanksgiving let your requests
be made known unto God

While I was employed with the outpatient center, Billy developed a problem with blocked arteries in his neck. The radiologist at the center had me bring him in for x-rays and an ultrasound. After reading the film they suggested we see a surgeon in Orlando who specialized in arterial obstruction. They called and were able to get him an appointment the same day. Surgery was scheduled and was successfully completed within the week.

In March a routine checkup revealed a large aneurysm in the aorta. Another surgery with greater risks brought about my decision to retire from secular work. It was a move I never regretted. The years that followed proved to be the most difficult.

CHAPTER XXIV

Challenging Changes

In 2003, while coming down the steps of the baptistery Billy fell breaking his hip. He was alone at the time and was found several hours later. An ambulance came and he was admitted to the local hospital. Surgery was scheduled for the next day. Intense suffering ultimately led him to ICU and continued for days. It was a very difficult time for all of the family. A case worker was brought in who later proved to be a blessing. Peggy was a former nurse and a Christian. She took a real interest in Billy and worked hard to get a positive recovery for him. He was released for home care and physical therapy. For three months he walked with a walker or cane. His pain never subsided. We decided to go for a second opinion. The new physician took x-rays and discovered the hip had never healed. He operated again and he said the pins and plate actually fell out on the table. They had never attached to his body and he had been walking around on a broken hip for three months. It was obvious that he had a high tolerance for pain.

After the second surgery his strength regained rapidly. He continued to preach although aided by a stool to support him. His endurance is unequalled to anyone I have ever known. People would ask him, "Preacher, when are you going to retire?" His reply: "When my toes stick up in the casket!" And that he did.

Months after Billy recovered; Bro. Steve Tucker came to me. He said, "Ms. Jean if you had your wishes, what would you like to do." I didn't even have to think about it. "I would like to go on an Alaskan cruise with Charles Stanley and the In Touch Ministries." A few months later I entered church on Sunday morning to a huge sign: "Preacher's Wife Sunday". A complete surprise, the members declared a day to celebrate their preacher's wife. The close of the service brought a gift for a ten day cruise to Alaska with a bouquet of roses for me and a captain's hat for Billy. I can truthfully say, I was overwhelmed with the love bestowed upon me that day. Humbled by the comments shared on my behalf I lay my head upon my pillow and thanked my loving heavenly Father.

Lamentations 3:24, 25
The Lord is my portion, saith my soul;
therefore willI hope in him.
The Lord is good unto them that wait for him,
to the soul that seeketh him. Psalm 37:4
Delight thyself also in the Lord, and he shall
give thee the desires of thine heart.

Our trip to Alaska was a dream come true. Our children, Lisa, and Michael, accompanied us on the cruise. Flying out of Orlando, we arrived in Seattle Washington six hours later. Accommodations were first class and we rested in our luxurious surroundings. The next day we boarded our ship.

The cruise was the last memorable trip we experienced together.

CHAPTER XXV

God Answered Our Prayers

In March of 2007 as he was helping with the laundry, Billy fell and broke his other hip. Some neighbors and friends helped me get him to the hospital. Another hip surgery was performed. Severe complications and a stroke followed. His days were spent in Orlando Regional hospital in the ICU unit on a respirator. The attending physician called me aside to sign a no resuscitation form. How do you make that choice? They had decided to take him off the ventilator but did not know the consequence.

It was Sunday morning Lisa and AnaRae were with me. Immediately after the doctor left us, I asked Lisa to call Bro. Jim Callen our associate pastor. They were about to enter the sanctuary for morning worship service. She called and the rest is history. Bro. Jim called the congregation to come forward for prayer. Later I was told it was a prayer meeting like never before. People were weeping and begging God to spare their preachers life and HE did. A week before this incident occurred, Brother Jim came to me with a scripture that God had given him.

St. John 11:4: When Jesus heard that (Lazarus was sick),
he said, This sickness is not unto death,
but for the glory of God,
that the Son of God might be glorified thereby.

He felt that Billy was going to recover and the scripture confirmed his thoughts.

During the long stay in the hospital the members graciously agreed to pay for room and board for me. There was a restored home near the hospital with rooms for families with loved ones who were in critical care. This was a blessing to me.

One evening as I left his room I felt an overwhelming sadness. I felt alone and it seemed that I had no peace. With tears streaming down my face, I walked back to a waiting room filled with anxious people. As I entered the hall, I noticed four volunteers. One was a beautiful Hispanic lady who looked at me and smiled. I tried smiling back through my tears when she turned and came directly to me. Reaching in her pocket she pulled out a small, New Testament. She said to me, "God told me to give this to you." Surprisingly she said, "You will find your peace." How did she know? Who was she? I never saw her again, but I believe God sent her to me. Her countenance was as if she had been with God.

While I was staying in Orlando, I met a lady who was experiencing the same situation. Her husband was at the point of death. She was alone. I ministered to her, and before I left, gave her the Bible that was given to me.

There is an old hymn that comes back to me. It is called "No, Never Alone". No never alone, No never alone, He promised never to leave me, Never to leave me alone. In every situation in life God has ministered to me through someone. He knows your need and He knows who you need. It is always the right person with the right words. It is my heart's desire that God will use me to be that right person for someone, somewhere that needs me.

Billy came home, but he was never the same again. His body weak, his spirit low but he never wanted to give up preaching. I watched as he struggled to dress himself and my heart ached for him. He was a proud man and so independent. He added a walking cane to his accessories but he refused a wheel chair unless it was absolutely necessary.

In June we celebrated our 50th wedding anniversary. The girls planned a party for us on Sunday Afternoon. Virginia Heyne and her sister Beth made a beautiful cake for us. The Fellowship Hall was decorated with Our Wedding Pictures. My gown was displayed on a mannequin, though yellow from age it reminded me of how much weight I had gained in 50 years. Billy was frail and had lost so much weight during his illness. The pictures we made were reflective of the sickness he had been through. It was a sad reminder to me of that good looking, black haired, eyes of steel man that I married. It broke my heart to see him struggling to speak and carry out his duties as a minister.

But he was still my knight in shining armor. He never lost my chain of thought while preaching. He could keep me spellbound. He always gave me a helping hand in the dishpan. He saw that the car was in immaculate condition. His concern was always about his family not himself.

We took a trip to Washington, D.C. Our grandson Adam was performing with the U.S. Navy Band. Adam graduated from Florida State University with a degree in Music. He was offered a position with the Navy Sea Chanters. Adam grew up loving music. He played the piano, violin and trombone in high school. At Florida State he played with the Marching Chiefs. In 2009 he joined the Navy and after basic training in Maryland he was stationed in D.C. permanently.

Before he left for D.C. his papa said to him, "Son, you go to Washington and you sing "Amazing Grace" to that bunch." And that he did! In September of 2010 he sang a solo for the September 11th memorial service at the Pentagon. It was televised nationwide and we sat at home and listened to Adam singing "Amazing Grace" to the entire nation and abroad. God helped to fulfill Papa's request.

It was a difficult trip for Billy to D.C. But he wanted to hear Adam sing in the United States Navy's Anniversary celebration. It was held in the historic Daughters of Revolution Hall in city center. The weather was typical October temperature. It was cold and rained the entire three days we were there. Mike and Lisa helped push Billy in the wheelchair that he despised. We rode the inner city subway which was a nightmare getting on and off. Adam and Jay Jones (visiting from Florida) met us for dinner at an exclusive restaurant downtown. It was raining so hard when we finished that Mike and Lisa called a taxi to take us to the concert. It was a hilarious ride down the inner city streets as I had fallen into the taxi on top of Billy. He was trying to get me off and we couldn't understand a word the taxi driver was saying. Eventually we arrived to meet Lisa and Mike just in time to get our tickets. The acoustics in that old building were astounding. The building was packed with veterans from each branch of the armed forces. As we stood that night and paid homage to our country our hearts were pounding with excitement. Our little grandson that proudly played the shepherd boy in Christmas pageants and sang in the church choir now performing in the Capitol City!

January 9th of 2009 our first grandchild, Aaron, married Heather Monteith. It would be the last family member that papa would join in matrimony. Heather, a native of Maine, endured constant teasing from Papa. We soon learned to love our new granddaughter. She has been a blessing to our family.

God graciously gave us our Pastor, Father, Friend and husband for three years after his bout with death. However they were not joyous years for him. His only joy was when he was behind the pulpit proclaiming the word of God. There were times people told me they could see a halo over him. God honors faithful preachers and he was faithful. His body racked with aches and pains, his steps slow and unsteady he remained faithful to his Lord.

We received a call from Dr. McAllister, president of Emmaus Baptist College. He wanted to visit the church. When he arrived that day he presented Billy with an Honorary Doctorate of Divinity. His years of service for the Lord were recognized by the school he had attended in Lakeland, Florida.

Billy wanted to make a trip back to his home in Alabama. By this time he was unable to drive due to the loss of his peripheral vision. I think the loss of his ability to drive was the last straw for him. If I ever drove him during our 52 years of marriage it was absolute necessity. He wanted to be in the driver's seat at all times. So.......I took him back to his old stomping grounds. In Gadsden, Alabama we drove past his mom and dad's home near the Coosa River. In Attalla, Alabama we saw Ma and Aunt Ada's little white house and porch still standing. We traveled up the mountain to Albertville where he was born and a visit with Bobby and Sue Bright. His brother Earl and family near Huntsville eagerly awaited our company. Having lost his middle brother

Gerald to cancer earlier, Earl was the closest relative left. Our visit was short but he was satisfied to see everyone. He reminisced along the way and showed me where he attended high school. He loved the mountains and scenery of Alabama, but he never wanted to go back there to live. When we married I was sure we would end up there one day. But he fell in love with Florida and it became home to him. I am sure God put that love in his heart because that was where HE wanted him to live. The trip was long and very taxing on both of us. What we did not know was that he was developing heart failure.

We arrived home and several days later, Billy's breathing became labored. He was diagnosed with congestive heart failure. Several bouts of severe weakness and breathing difficulty brought hospitalization. This went on for weeks.

In June he seemed to be getting better. We talked about taking a short trip for our 52nd anniversary. There was a quaint place near our girls called Crystal River. We found a hotel with rooms looking over the river. It was set up for us to leave on Tuesday, but before we could leave, we had to attend a funeral. It was just one of those preacher prerequisites. After saying good-bye to our associate pastor and friends we hasted to get out of town. My good-byes were to not call to us; we are going on a second honeymoon!

On the way to Crystal River, Billy asked me a strange question. He said, "If anything should happen to me, you wouldn't marry a preacher would you?" "No way!" I replied emphatically. Then he asked, "You wouldn't move in with the girls, would you?" What a strange thing this was for him to ask me these unusual questions. He never spoke to me about his passing and what I would or wouldn't do. "Well, I never thought about it," I replied. "Well you do not want to be a burden to those girls!" he answered.

Tuesday evening AnaRae, Jeff and Mary Hannah took us to a seafood restaurant on the River. Billy loved oysters, and he ate with heartiness. It was good to see him enjoy eating and having a good laugh with his family. The next day they came over to enjoy a swim in the pool. Mary Hannah announced she was going to cook dinner for us.

We were met that evening by Lily Belle, the Jack Russell family pet. Papa took a chair in the living room. The dog never left his side. A bit unusual as papa had a come and go relationship with Lily. We enjoyed our meal and family time watching old videos of our little princess.

Thursday morning around six o'clock I was awakened by Billy struggling, almost panting for breath. I knew the sound, just weeks before we had to call the paramedics to come for the same issue. I reached for the phone and called 911. Then I called the front desk of the hotel to see where the nearest hospital was located. It was serious; I knew we were in trouble. She came and stayed with me until the paramedics arrived. The hospital was only five miles away. They took him, and I got directions. The last time I went through this at home I had dropped to my knees and prayed God please don't take him, I need him. This time, I dropped to my knees but with a grieving heart, I prayed God, Thy will be done. It was a hard prayer, but I could not stand to see him suffer.

A quick call to Lisa and AnaRae brought them to my side at the hospital within the hour. We waited. Finally the on call physician called us in to talk. "He is very critical, "he said. "Our only choice is to put him on life support." The three of us wept. How can we do this to him again? He had voiced his opinion after his last bout with a ventilator. "Do not ever do this to me again" he had said. The three of us went into an adjacent room and prayed. "God show us what to do, he did not want this, and we would have to sign papers again. Can we do it? Should we do it? Before we could make up our minds about what to do, they called us back. He is slipping, his face already ashen gray we could barely understand his words. As I caressed his hand and face, he tried to speak and held up his fingers indicating a five and two. I tried to repeat what I thought he was saying. He would shake his head, no. Then AnaRae on his left said, "Mama, he is telling you, thank you for fifty two years." He nodded yes. He knew he was going. It was the last words he spoke. My man, my dream, my lover, my friend and companion, gone, gone, gone. He drifted off quietly into another world, a place of joy, a place of contentment, a heavenly home, his new home. At last he is with the God he has preached of and His Son who gave His life for him. A little farm boy raised the poorest of the poor now in a mansion walking streets of gold. He always said he wanted to live on the corner of Glory and Halleluiah Avenue next to Dr. B. R. Lakin. I believe he was greeted by his precious mother, Johnnie and hosts of friends and relatives. But, most of all I believe he will receive a Crown of Righteousness for his faithfulness to Jesus.

CHAPTER XXVI

The Funeral

Never in my wildest dreams would I have expected the massive number of people who paid their respects. The viewing was on Saturday night and I stood until I trembled for four hours greeting people. I was told they were lined up for blocks around the church.

He had jokingly told me one day that when he died he wanted a red casket. Knowing how much he loved the color red I knew he would be pleased. Red is not an ordinary casket color but his friends Roger Thompson and Bill Cool did their best to find one. Billy had two great friends in these men that he had worked with for years in the funeral home.

People from across the nation came and paid their respects. The line was long, their hearts sincere; they blessed me by coming.

Famous NFL football and baseball player, John Bramlett had been scheduled to speak for us that week end. His longtime friend Tracy Bond was a member of our congregation. We often entertained John and Tracy in our home and had planned to on this weekend. Billy had given our grandson Nate a tape and book about "The Bull" John's nickname. Nate had fallen in love with his story, sharing it with friends and his coach in Nevada. Billy said he wanted to get a baseball and have John sign it for Nate. Billy didn't get to buy the ball but to our surprise, John Bramlett attended the funeral and gave a signed baseball to our grandson Nate.

Now in heaven John Bramlett will forever be remembered by our family for his respect and kindness.

Sunday morning worship hour was performed with the preacher laid out in his red casket. A black suit with a red tie and pocket kerchief adorned his stiff, cold body. But you see, he wasn't there, not in that casket but overhead from a heavenly view he watched as we said our last good-byes. Good bye to that preacher who doesn't need a cane or a wheelchair. He not only walks, he runs and perhaps dances down those golden streets with Peter, James and John. He doesn't preach to poor old lost souls any more but he praises the Jesus who saves them. He bows and sings praises to the King of Kings. He couldn't carry a tune down here but hopefully he is on key up there.

We used to laugh about his seminary days when he took a music class. The professor tried him out for the choir. He said Billy, go up the scale, do, re, mi, fa, then he said, go down the scale so, fa, mi, re, then he said: "Son, you do have a problem."

Good Bye World, Good Bye were the familiar words heard that morning from our choir. His favorite songs were sung or played that day. "Amazing Grace," "The King is coming," "Oh What a Savior" were fervently sung in his memory. Preachers and laymen spoke with sincerity that remains a lasting memory. They spoke of his legacy and of a hope that we would meet again. Our grandson Adam sang "Somebody's Coming" with his mom and dad and brother Aaron. It was an unusual Morning Worship hour for visitors that day. But, our family felt Sunday was appropriate for his last day at Eastern Avenue Baptist Church. There were few Sundays that he wasn't in church on Sunday morning and those were sick days. The service was just as he would have wanted, upbeat, joyful with praise to the heavenly Father.

The long journey to the cemetery was the hardest part. The American flag was presented to me by a young man that Billy loved. Travis Taylor, representing the U.S. Coast Guard, stood tall and handsome in his uniform. With tears streaming down his face he repeated the solemn statement: *This flag is presented on behalf of a grateful nation and the United States Coast Guard as a token of appreciation for your loved one's honorable and faithful service.*

Not only was he faithful to the United States Air Force but to his Lord and Savior, Jesus Christ.

CHAPTER XXVII

The Final Chapter

When reading back on my life's story, it sounds like someone's fairy tale life. There were hardships along the way. There is no perfect marriage but there is a truth to the statement: A family that prays together, Stays together.

I wish the wisdom that is mine today would have been with me from the beginning. Getting older does get one wiser but oh how I wish that could reverse. Foolish choices and decisions perhaps turn folly into wisdom. It is the learning process that is timely and difficult.

Some might say, what a boring life she lived: Listening to sermons Sunday after Sunday for fifty-two years. But you see they were sermons that came from the man I loved. I knew how he lived every day. I knew how he treated his neighbor. I knew the heartache he carried from childhood. I knew how his father belittled him and told him he would never amount to anything. Yes, I loved his sermons, all of them, good and bad. They told the story of salvation every one of them. There was one time in his ministry that he failed to give an invitation to the lost. After church Junior Hansell came to him and said, Preacher, I was going to give my heart to Jesus tonight. Billy took him in his office and led him to the Lord immediately. But, he never again failed to give an invitation.

It has been four and ½ years now since his death. There is not a single day that goes by that I do not miss him. I could always count on his laughter, his stories that I knew by heart, his presence at the Sunday dinner table and his advice. He was the decision maker around our house. There are times now that I scream, "Billy, what do I do?" There is no answer but later that still small voice from within whispers, "Listen my child, I will lead you."

How good it is to know the Lord. How precious is His presence in my daily life. It is my desire that you will be blessed from hearing my story.

"There is only one life, it too shall pass, and only what is done for Christ will last."

My Three Girls

ABOUT THE AUTHOR

Emma Jean Rigsby has been a pastor's wife for fifty-two years. After the death of her husband, Billy, she determined to share her life as a preacher's wife. She was inspired by a book, "How to be a Preacher's Wife and Like it" written in the 1940's. The book was initially written for her children to have a glimpse into her past. However, due to requests from friends and family it will be available to those interested in the life experiences of people in ministry.

Printed in the United States
By Bookmasters